ADORABLE ANIMAL STORIES TO BRIGHTEN YOUR DAY

This edition first published in Great Britain in 2016 by Carlton Books Ltd
20 Mortimer Street
London W1T 3JW

A CIP catalogue for this book is available from the British Library.

ISBN 978-1-78097-879-6

Printed in Dubai

Previously published as *The Dog that Survived the Titanic* in 2012

10 9 8 7 6 5 4 3 2 1

ADORABLE ANIMAL STORIES TO BRIGHTEN YOUR DAY

500 incredible but
true animal tales

WRITTEN BY ROBERT LODGE

CARLTON
BOOKS

Conversation between the publisher and Bill Oddie.

Mr Oddie, what – or rather who – we need to write a foreword is someone who is into animals, but also into comedy.

Not a lot of choice there then. So, is this a book about animals, or is it meant to be funny?

*It isn't **meant** to be funny. It **is** funny.*

So, it's laughing at animals. I'm not sure that's very good for my image.

No, no. It definitely is not laughing at animals.

Oh. Why not? Some of them are extremely funny. I laugh at them all the time. One glimpse of a baboon's bottom and I'm away! And have you ever seen a baby cormorant? Talk about ugly! And dogs! Now dogs really are funny. My next door neighbour has a spaniel that makes me fall about laughing!

Got a silly face has he?

No no, he keeps telling really good jokes!

Really? You don't do comedy any more, do you? Look, are you going to do this foreword or not?

Probably, I just have a few stipulations.

Such as?

I can't condone any cruelty or humiliation. No zoos, menageries and definitely no circuses. No performing animals. And I'd like you to stress the therapeutic benefits of owning a pet, and the importance of knowing how to care for it. And of course I want a lot of wildlife, and I don't want it treated frivolously. I don't mind a few wry heart-warming anecdotes, but let's have lots of amazing statistics to balance them up. Like how many miles Arctic terns fly on migration or how far away elephants can hear each other.

Er, look Mr Oddie, I am not entirely certain that this is the kind of book you'd want to be associated with. Tell you what, why don't you read it?

What!? You've got to be kidding! People who write forewords never read the book.

You might like it.

Mmm, let's see... 'The dog that survived the *Titanic*.' Is that true? That's incredible. 'The cat that lived up a tree for six years.' Best place for it I'd say. A gorilla learning sign language. They are so intelligent! A bald chimp! A short-sighted sheep! That's funny. Any snake stories? Ferrets? Rats? Hey, I really like this!

So you will write the foreword?

Certainly.

Foreword by Bill Oddie

This a good book.

Bill Oddie

Introduction by Robert Lodge

Animals have always been a part of my working and personal life. As a one-time smallholder aiming for self-sufficiency I have seen foals, calves, kittens, puppies and piglets go from birth to thriving full growth and marvelled at the process and the traits they develop. Then, as a journalist I would be forever reporting on incredible animal stories as the public couldn't seem to get enough of them.

Animals are full of quirks and mysteries but they get on very well all by themselves. During the writing of this book it struck me more and more that it is the introduction of the human element that elevates these creatures' lives into the realms of the bizarre, in which many of these stories reside. This book is filled with amazing displays of animals' courage, kindness and determination and this makes me think even more how honoured we are to share the planet with them.

Much of the writing was completed through a cold winter and I owe a debt to an animal for it. Billy, my faithful Irish Wheaten terrier, spent many dozing hours under my desk, offering quiet inspiration – and keeping my feet warm!

Robert Lodge

Dogged Titanic Survivor

A dog that survived the tragic sinking of *RMS Titanic* in 1912 actually helped to save lives. But for Rigel, the giant Newfoundland, the death toll of 1,517 people when the ship quickly sank after hitting an iceberg in the North Atlantic Ocean would have been higher. Rigel, who belonged to the *Titanic's* First Officer, spent three hours in the icy ocean and was instrumental in alerting the rescue ship *RMS Carpathia* to a boatload of survivors. The exhausted survivors in their lifeboat had drifted dangerously under the *Carpathia's* starboard bow but were close to the steamship and in danger of being run down until Rigel, who was swimming ahead of the craft, let rip a volley of sharp barks. This alerted the *Carpathia* lookouts and evasive action was taken and the survivors and Rigel were brought on board. The Newfoundland showed no ill effects as a result of his time in the icy water and was later adopted by *Carpathia* crewman Jonas Briggs.

Chimp My Ride

A popular tourist attraction in the French port city of Marseille at the turn of the century was a chimpanzee called Henri, which rode a motorcycle. He also offered lifts on the pillion seat – an offer only taken up by the bravest.

Jumbo Law

Getting an elephant onto an aptly named "Jumbo" jet could prove a problem because it's illegal to walk an elephant through the approach tunnel to London's Heathrow Airport.

Canine Wedding

Two tiny dogs were "married" in a ceremony that set an owner back £20,000 ($30,000) in 2011. Louise Harris, from Bradwell-on-Sea in Essex, England, ran an online competition to find a "groom" for her Yorkshire terrier Lola and from the hundreds of responses she picked Mugly, a Chinese Crested dog. The wedding and reception in the grounds of a mansion were so pricy because Lola wore a £1,000 ($1,500) specially designed dress sporting 1,800 Swarovski crystals. Mugly looked resplendent in a tuxedo and top hat.

Crazy Mixed-Up Crow

A crow chick hand-reared by a family in Germany grew up with a dachshund dog as a companion and developed some very canine traits: barking and rolling over to have his tummy tickled.

Chocs Away!

A Spanish police sniffer dog got it all wrong when a suspicious parcel was found in a courtroom in Palma, Majorca in 2011. The mystery package held a box of chocolates and the dog, normally so disciplined, couldn't contain itself and promptly wolfed the lot. Understandably miffed, the local police chief sent the renegade sniffer for retraining.

PoW Pup

A dog was officially recognized as a prisoner of the Japanese during World War II. Prisoner 81A was an English pointer called Judy, who became a symbol of hope and courage for Allied troops imprisoned and tortured in the Far East. She also saved countless lives by alerting troops to hostile aircraft and protecting them against scorpions, poisonous snakes and brutal prison guards. Shanghai-born Judy was a Royal Navy mascot on *HMS Grasshopper* when, in 1942, the gunboat was torpedoed and sunk. With more than 120 crew Judy made it to an uninhabited island which had no water – until Judy sniffed out a freshwater spring. Eventually they were all captured and sent to the Gloergoer camp in Medan, Indonesia, where Leading Aircraftsman Frank Williams began sharing his daily handful of maggoty boiled rice with her. Judy became the camp darling because she sounded the alarm if scorpions, snakes or guards came near. When prisoners were dragged away for brutal beatings, she would intervene – barking, snarling and attacking the guards. She was constantly hunted by the guards but evaded capture until Williams persuaded a drunk camp commandant to sign papers that made her an official PoW. Despite many privations Judy survived her war ordeal and was repatriated to Britain where in 1946 her exploits earned her the Dickin Medal – the Victoria Cross equivalent for animal bravery.

Pork Talk

A pig called Felix cheered up elderly people by visiting a care home in Gelsenkirchen, Germany. Staff said being visited by Felix and his farmer owner instead of pet dogs sparked curiosity and conversation in the senior citizens.

Lion Around

Andre Potgeiter's bed was pretty crowded. He and his wife Talita had to budge up to make room for a 160kg (25st) lion. Storm, the lion they took in after it was abandoned by its mother in 2007, slept on their bed from the start and stayed on as a bedmate when she was fully grown. The lion, which made friends with the couple's meerkat, zebra and three great dane dogs, also liked to bath with Talita and shower with Andre.

Flock & Awe

Border collie Ci suffered the ignominy of being branded Britain's worst sheepdog – because sheep scared him. The four-year-old had been terrified of sheep since he was a puppy and when he tried to round them up in the fields around his home in Somerset, England, they ganged up on him. A video of Ci feeling in terror was a YouTube hit in 2011.

Pointer's Point

A pointer dog named Don surprised – and mystified – German scientists in the 1930s by mimicking the human voice to bark the words: "Hungry. Give me cakes!" The boffins were unsure why this pointer could achieve such an unusual trait.

Cock-A-Doodle, Shoo!

Barry the cockerel's celebratory morning crows of 2011 were not appreciated by children taking their exams in Cambridge, England. They were so distracting, the school asked his owners (a care home) to send Barry on an enforced holiday for two weeks.

Spurs Pleased as a Parrot

A parrot spent 11 pampered years at the stadium home of English football club Tottenham Hotspur. The team had made a pioneering trip to Argentina and Uruguay in 1908 and on the long voyage back, two players were presented with the parrot for winning a fancy dress competition as pirates. Thereafter, its home was at the White Hart Lane ground, though it failed to replace the gamecock on the club badge.

Naughty Kitty!

Forget having a ball of wool or a toy to play with, Speedy the cat was into bras and knickers. The three-year-old moggy turned washing-line raider in Wiesendangen, Switzerland and displayed a distinct preference for ladies' lingerie. Police were stumped following the outbreak of washing-line thefts. Eventually, Speedy's owner turned him in after she kept finding underwear in her kitchen that was not hers.

Old Goldfish

Tish the goldfish lived just long enough to establish himself as the world's oldest captive goldfish in 1999 – before expiring peacefully in his bowl, 43 years after he was won as a prize at a funfair. He was recognized by Guinness World Records in 1998 but was later found dead at the bottom of his bowl after a short illness. Tish was buried with full honours in a yoghurt carton in the garden of his owner, Hilda Hand.

Rodent Chic

New Yorker Ada Nieves created just the thing for the raffish rat about town in 2011. She launched a range of designer clothes for rodents. The range of "rat couture" included tuxedos, frocks and even wedding dresses, which she claimed make your pet rat look "cute". The rodent gear followed an already-established trend for dressing dogs and pet pigs in couture clothes.

Watership Hound?

A labrador retriever foraging for lizards returned home with a pair of wild baby rabbits and adopted them! Koa of San Francisco, California took on the role of mother in 2011. She kept the youngsters safe and warm in the crook of her leg and allowed the bunnies to hop all over her. Experts say because Koa has never had puppies, she believes the rabbits are her own offspring.

Falling Fella

Voodoo, a Manx cat who lived life on the edge, fell 34 storeys from an apartment balcony in Australia and survived with nothing more than a few scratches. The miracle cat, a breed which has no tail, limped home with a bloodshot eye, scratched ear, cut mouth and damaged paw.

Penguin Boot's a Shoe-In

It ranked as one of the most bizarre phone calls, even for California. A caller rang a shoemaker to ask for a boot… for a penguin. And this was a genuine call, from staff at Santa Barbara Zoo in the USA, who had a lame penguin and needed a specially built up boot. After it was fitted, the penguin waddled off happily, living up to his name of Lucky!

Sea Elephants

In 2011, the world's only ocean-going elephants were finally retired. The last pair of 10 sea-swimming elephants was put out to pasture after 40 years of ferrying logs between the Andaman and Nicobar Islands in the Indian Ocean. While elephants love water and are good swimmers, the 10 had to be specially trained to swim in seawater. They soon became a popular tourist attraction and often took to the crystal-clear waters with scuba divers and snorkellers.

Cat Life – Presidential Style

Socks, the black-and-white cat adopted by the family of former US President Bill Clinton, became famous in his own right. During the eight-year Clinton administration from 1983-91, he was used to host the children's version of the White House website.

Every Little Peck Helps

A sparrow trapped in a supermarket took out his frustration on shoppers by divebombing them in the aisles. Managers at the Tesco store in Bedford, England, were forced to call in pest controllers, who caught the trapped bird and set it free in 2011.

Mane Chance

Christian the lion cub became one of the most-famous icons of the "Swinging Sixties" in London, England and was even purchased from top people's store Harrods in the days when that was legal. He lived in a flat in Chelsea's fashionable King's Road with Australian-born friends, John Rendall and Anthony "Ace" Bourke, and was taken to parties and restaurants in the back of a Mercedes Cabriolet. In 1971 when Christian grew too big, John and Anthony took him to Africa to the home of celebrated conservationist George Adamson of *Born Free* fame, where Christian was rehabilitated and freed into a reserve. Years later when John and Anthony revisited the reserve, Christian recognized them in a joyful reunion. The friends' experiences with Christian spawned a bestselling book.

Skateboard Terrier Terror

Bodhi the skateboarding dog was collared for causing a public nuisance and cost his owner £80 ($130). With his skilful skateboarding, the Lakeland terrier was a freewheeling star attraction in the English seaside town of Brighton until 2011, when two women tripped over his skateboard. Bodhi's owner Jonathan Fell fell foul of the law because Bodhi was not on a lead and he was subsequently fined for not keeping his dog under control. This didn't mean Bodhi had to dismount for good, however, because he was still free to skateboard in local parks.

Doggy Seal

A fearless dog was a member of the Navy Seals assault team that stormed Al-Qaeda leader and founder Osama Bin Laden's secret lair in Pakistan in 2011. The explosive-sniffing dog was strapped to a team member as they captured and killed the evil mastermind behind the 9/11 attacks in New York. The fearless creature (who like his human teammates remains anonymous) was lowered down a rope from a helicopter into Bin Laden's hideout in the town of Abbottabad. Heavily armoured dogs of war used in such top-secret operations are equipped with infrared night-sight cameras and wear body armour to withstand shrapnel, bullets and knives.

Octopus Oracle

An octopus became the unlikely star of the 2010 football World Cup… for predicting match results. Paul the psychic octopus maintained a 100 per cent success rate at the South Africa tournament by correctly predicting Spain's victory over the Netherlands in the final. Staff at the Sea Life aquarium at Oberhausen, Germany devised a game in which Paul was offered the choice of two glass boxes containing a mussel. It was noted on almost every occasion, the team that Paul's tentacle touched first went on to win their match. He correctly guessed the outcome of all Germany's group games as well as the country's semi-final defeat.

Bear-ly Tolerant

Celebrities sick of being hounded by the paparazzi had much to learn in 2010 from a polar bear which objected to being photographed. Three wildlife photographers had to run for it after the hacked-off bear grabbed their tripod and ran off with it into the snowy wastes of Barter Island, Alaska.

Leisurely Meal

A microbe discovered in 2010 will be on iron rations for some time to come. *Halomonas titanicae* was found for the first time feeding off the rusting hulk of the disaster liner *RMS Titanic* lying 3.8km (2.3 miles) below the surface of the Atlantic Ocean. The microbes were feeding off the oxidizing iron but it will be a long meal as the *Titanic*, which sank at the cost of 1,517 lives after hitting an iceberg in 1912, was 269m (882ft) long and weighed 46,000 tons.

No Eggs, Please

Red kites developed a love for a full English breakfast at a roadside café in England. The birds, once almost extinct in the country, descended in their dozens on the café at Fen Ditton, Cambridgeshire because the owner put out bacon, sausages and bread and butter for them. He was never insensitive enough to put out scrambled eggs, of course.

Life in the Fast Lane

A death-defying marmot with no sense of fear gave drivers a heck of a shock in suddenly popping its head up from a pothole in the road. The fearless fur-ball belied its name – the yellow-bellied marmot – by dicing with death and only ducking its head at the last moment as cars on a stretch of road in Montana, USA, hurtled over it.

Pop-Star Blackbird

Blackbirds hit the top of birdsong charts in 2011. Their song was voted best for de-stressing and lifting the spirits in a 2011 Top 10 by users of the online Pure/Birdsong library aimed at helping people to identify birds in their garden or park. The blackbird was a "real tweet" for an overwhelming number of listeners, with the blue tit second and the black-headed gull third. The rest of the bird chart top five was made up by the bullfinch and robin respectively.

Buzzard Buzzed

London's immigration issues spread to the bird world in 2011, when police had to be called in to sort out a punch-up. Seagulls took exception to a buzzard, Britain's largest bird of prey and rarely seen in London, appearing on their turf and tried to send it off. Enter the Metropolitan Police's Marine Unit, which saw the buzzard in distress and being dive-bombed near Westminster Bridge. After repeated attempts at a rescue the buzzard was wrapped in a blanket and later released on the city outskirts, which were more conducive to its countryside environment.

Klepto-Cat

Dusty the cat couldn't keep his paws to himself when it came to other people's property in 2010–11. The five-year-old prolific cat burglar stoles hundreds of gloves, towels, shoes and swimsuits from homes around San Mateo, California and often raided the same ones twice in a night.

Taste For the High Life

A rottweiler dog with a head for heights had England's firemen on the hop in 2011. The runaway squeezed through the window of a house at Basildon, Essex and was spotted trapped on a roof. Firemen were called to bring him back down to earth; then two hours later they were back. Like the proverbial old dog not learning new tricks, the rottie had done it all over again and was back on the roof!

Basket Hangover

Daisy the duck wanted the high life for her chicks in 2011 and took over a pub's hanging flower basket as a nest. She laid six eggs in the basket at the City of London pub in Dymchurch, England and duly sat on them, surveying the crowds who turned up to watch her.

Downhill Diversion

Olympic skiers were amazed when a lynx trotted across the slopes just before the 2010 Winter Games Men's Downhill event was due to begin in Whistler, British Columbia, Canada.

Sinning Saint Bernard?

Arthur the dog's sainthood didn't shield him from accusations of being a bank robber in 2009. The 92kg (203lb) St Bernard caused panic at Locksbottom, England when he bolted through the doors of a bank and spooked customers. Staff thought the commotion meant a robbery was taking place and promptly put emergency procedures into action. Arthur was mystified why, on his appearance, shutters clanked into place, automatic locks clicked home and police raced to the scene – he was just being his usual friendly self!

Apeing the Expert

A crested black macaque proved a fast learner after a wildlife photographer left his camera unattended. When David Slater got back to his gear in the Indonesian rainforest in 2011, the macaque had mastered the operation of a Canon EOS 5D and snapped hundreds of shots, including a self-portrait and members of its peer group.

Mice Place to Live

A platform machine proved just the ticket for Britain's rarest mammals. Four *Glis glis* dormice made a nest in a railway station ticket machine at Aylesbury, Buckinghamshire in 2011 but in a cruel twist of irony, their nest led to them becoming almost homeless. It caused the machine to malfunction and engineers had to move the family to a local animal hospital while repairs were made.

Hearty Show

An emperor penguin chick was found in the Antarctic in 2011 with a perfectly shaped white heart on his black breast plumage.

Flippin' Good!

Charlie the seal showed he was brighter than most of his species by learning how to wave to curious onlookers with his flipper. Crowds, who flocked in 2011 to Howth Harbour, near Dublin in the Republic of Ireland, got a wave from crafty Charlie – if they threw food. But he was not immune to professional jealousy after getting more food than the rest of the seals in the harbour and suffered a few envious bites.

Thanks, Mate!

Onlookers at an English coastal town were amazed when a golden labrador spotted a small dog struggling out at sea, dived in and pushed it back to safety with her nose.

Chain of Love

Six men roped themselves together to save a dog from drowning in one of the most treacherous storms ever to hit Cornwall in England. Mousse the spaniel had already cheated death when the French trawler she was on sank in a huge storm in 1995. Local villagers, who had turned out to watch the rescue of the trawler crew by helicopters, became fascinated by Mousse's struggles in the sea. The six strong men roped themselves together and risked their own lives until a weakening Mousse came within their grasp and she was hauled to safety to make a full recovery.

Rich Food

Barney the puppy wasn't letting on where he had hidden a diamond ring for which his family were frantically searching in their home. While they turned their house in Nottinghamshire, England upside down hunting for a valuable heirloom, Barney calmly looked on, unconcerned… until they ran a metal detector over him. The hungry hound had swallowed the sparklers and needed an operation to save his life – and retrieve the stolen goods!

Playing in Stripes

Serbian football team Obilic Belgrade showed they meant business in 2011 by letting their baby tiger mascot loose onto the pitch before games. Experienced tiger handlers were close by to make sure the tigers didn't leap into the crowd.

Small Bumps in the Road?

The French really love snails for more than escargots on restaurant menus. In various parts of the country, signs have been spotted warning drivers of snails crossing the road.

He Nose, You Know

A search dog used to find people trapped in the rubble during the London Blitz had a real nose for the job. In 1941, Jet – who won the highest medal for dogs, the Dickin Medal, for his work – discovered 25 people trapped under a bombed building.

Sheep High Life

A short-sighted sheep had to be rescued from the roof of a house. The lost sheep spent 40 minutes in 2011 on the sloping tiles of a house in Pontycymer, near Bridgend, South Wales, which backs onto a hill. It appears the sheep wandered off the hill onto a flat-roofed bathroom extension and then the pitched roof of the house, where he seemed more comfortable on the angled tiles than his Fire Brigade rescuers. The animal was unhurt.

Pocket Pony

A pony called Einstein claimed the title of the Smallest Stallion in the World in 2011 when, as a yearling, he measured just 50cm (20in). People queued up to see him when he was born weighing only 2.7kg (6lb) on a farm at Barnstead, New Hampshire.

Nest Toll

Bell-ringing at an English country church was suspended by a family of jackdaws, who had made their nest close to one of its bells in 2011. Ringers at St Mary the Virgin Church in Hadleigh, Suffolk took a break while the eggs hatched and chicks fledged.

San Fran-stinko

Amorous skunks thought the answer to their mating prayers was in the US city of San Francisco in the spring of 2012. Hundreds of the creatures flooded the California city, stinking the place out!

White Lightning

An escaped albino ostrich broke the speed limit by sprinting at more than 40mph through an English port town in 2011. The giant bird legged it along roads with 30mph limits with six police officers in pursuit. A passing driver used deft skills to carefully herd the 2m (6.5ft) tall ostrich into a car park, where he "parked" it until police and animal experts caught up and duly "arrested" the speeder.

Make It Snappy!

A 6m (20ft) crocodile became a favourite with boatloads of camera-wielding tourists by launching its huge bulk completely out of the water as they sailed by. Lured by food at the end of the pole, Brutus – who was thought to be 80 years old in 2011 – belied his venerable years to rocket out of the water near Darwin, Australia in a spectacular leap that thrilled audiences.

Dog Knows Best

The uncanny senses of a guard dog sniffed out a spy during the Napoleonic Wars. A trained French poodle living with a regiment of French Grenadiers acted out of character when a messenger arrived and began growling and snarling at him. The poodle had to be restrained but it was only later that it was discovered that the man was a spy for enemy Austrians. Vindicated, the dog was allowed to follow the spy and lead a pursuit of him, which led to his capture.

Bit of Luck

A dog called Bryn is probably the only animal ever credited with saving a football club from relegation. The Torquay United team (from Devon, England) was playing on the last day of the 1986–87 season and faced being dropped altogether from the English Football League. With Torquay trailing 2-1 to Crewe Alexandra, Bryn – a police dog patrolling the touchline with his handler – suddenly took it into his head to bite the thigh of Torquay player Jim McNichol. It took four minutes to treat the wound and it was ironically in the fourth minute of injury time that striker Paul Donson snatched a dramatic equalizer to save Torquay. Bryn's contribution didn't go unnoticed at the club. After his death from natural causes in retirement 10 years later he was stuffed and put on display in the Torquay boardroom.

Turtle Chaos

Everything stops for a turtle's need to breed – including one of the busiest airports in the world. Passengers at New York's JFK were delayed in 2011 when around 150 diamondback terrapin turtles were spotted crossing a runway. They were making a beeline for the nearest sandy beach to lay their eggs at Jamaica Bay Wildlife Refuge bordering JFK. Spotting the terrapins, measuring between 12.5-17.5cm (5-7in), pilots brought their giant jetliners to a halt, causing the runway to be temporarily shut down. Staff rushed onto the tarmac and helped the creatures on their way.

More Than a Mere Cat

Poppy the cross Maltese terrier-chihuahua dog came to the rescue of a bullied meerkat in England. Timon the meerkat had to be separated in 2011 from its own kind at a menagerie in Dronfield, Derbyshire because it was being savaged. John and Sally Bent introduced Timon to Poppy and they became inseparable friends, play-fighting and sharing a bath and a bed together.

Monkey Alert

A bald bug-eyed monkey caused an alien alert in China in 2011. The half-metre (20in) creature looked so strange when it was discovered in a flat in the village of Gezhai that callers claimed it was an alien from another world and wanted the police out in force. It turned out to be a malnourished baby monkey suffering from hair loss. The villagers decided to keep the "alien" and indulged its love of peaches.

Polite Parrot

There was no traditional bad language associated with talking parrots from Prudle the record breaking grey parrot. Owned by Iris Frost in Uganda where he was captured in 1958, grey parrot Prudle had a vocabulary of 800 words of polite conversation by her death in 1977. She said "good morning" on waking and "good night" before settling down for the evening. Prudle even politely asked to come out of her cage when she wanted to stretch her wings.

Toe Triumph

No one wanted to get clawed by Jake the cat. In 2002, the Canadian tabby was found to have 28 toes – 10 more than normal cats. Bet he went through scratching posts in no time at all!

Move Over, Michael Jackson

The manakin bird was moonwalking thousands of years before pop superstar Michael Jackson perfected the art. Indeed, the native of South America and the Caribbean islands dances to impress the ladies. The bird has become a YouTube video hit as he lifts his tail, takes little steps and, with slick footwork, slides à la Jackson along the branch of a tree.

Nesty Shock

Naturally, cats drag prey through their owners' cat flaps all the time but Bella, a moggy from Taunton in England, went a lot further in 2011. She pulled a whole nest containing three chicks into the house, where her owners had to act quickly to rescue the babies.

Leap Into Limelight

Socks the cat made a leap into history when he jumped into the arms of Chelsea Clinton at her piano teacher's house in Little Rock, Arkansas, USA in 1991. Socks, named because of his four white paws, was destined to be the "top cat" because he was adopted by Chelsea's parents, Bill and Hillary Clinton, who were to spend for eight years in the White House.

Cooked-Up Voice

The famous "voice" of Flipper in the films and TV series of the 1960s was actually the doctored song of a kookaburra – a large terrestrial kingfisher bird native to Australia and New Guinea.

Fat Chance!

Obesity is not always a bad thing – it can even be a lifesaver. A sheep which got lost in a blizzard in Aberdeenshire, Scotland in 1984 was buried up to its ears in a snowdrift for a month and a half. Found 45 days later after a thaw set in, the sheep was a lot thinner as she had lived off her own fat. Her farmer owner said she had been overweight and the fat reserves had saved her life.

New to Tweeting

A mouse that can sing like a bird was bred in 2010. The genetically-modified rodent was produced at a Japanese research laboratory but the vocal talent came about by accident. A researcher was checking a batch of new-born mice when one of them sang like a bird. Lead researcher Arikuni Uchimura said the object of the research was not to produce the first singing mouse to get to No. 1 in the pop charts but part of a wider project looking into how human language evolved.

Party Poo-per

Pigeons inadvertently led to the disappointment of thousands of rock fans in 2010. The Kings of Leon concert in St Louis, Missouri, USA had to be called off on safety grounds after a pigeon dropping landed on the head of bass guitarist Jared Followill.

Game, Set and Trap!

In a scene reminiscent of the Wild West, four loose horses brought havoc to a suburb of the Welsh capital Cardiff in 2011. But their freedom didn't last long as police herded them toward a tennis court in a local park and corralled them behind the high wire until their owners could be contacted.

Paul Feels Sheepish

In 2011, British comedian and TV presenter Paul O'Grady gave a home to a lamb that had been dumped in a garbage bin. O'Grady, who already had his own flock of sheep, volunteered to re-home the month-old lamb, named Winston, which was found among rubbish in Manchester, England. Winston received treatment for an ulcerated eye but was otherwise unharmed by his ordeal.

25-Second Star

A cat that appeared on British TV for just 25 seconds a week for more than 10 years attracted a 1,500-strong fan club. Frisky the tabby and white Tom was on screen for five seconds every time popular Granada TV soap Coronation Street aired between 1990 and 2001. He died, aged 14, of old age in 2000. In 2011, Frisky's cremated ashes were auctioned and the £844 ($1336) raised split among charities.

Woolly Thinking

Shrek the Merino sheep shot to international fame in 2004 after he avoided being caught and shorn for six years. Year after year, he made himself scarce when the shearers arrived at the New Zealand farm where he lived. The escape artist was finally caught in 2004 and his years of fleece disappeared in 20 minutes. The shearing of 27kg (60lb), broadcast on national TV, yielded enough wool to make 20 men's suits.

Elvis Hounded

Millions of female fans would have loved an audience with Elvis Presley during his singing career but a dog named Sherman managed to achieve this in 1956. It was Sherman's one claim to fame as nothing else has been recorded about the creature. His starring role came after the public outcry about Presley's gyrating dance while performing "Hound Dog" on the Milton Berle Show. A month later, TV executives on the Steve Allen Show wanted to avoid a similar incident and had Presley wearing a tuxedo and singing the same song to Sherman.

Mere Success

TV success for meerkats led to a spate of animal thefts in Britain during 2010 and 2011. Talking meerkats were the stars of the www.comparethemarket.com TV campaign, but the creatures proved so endearing that people tried to get their hands on them for real. Zoos and wildlife parks were forced to step up security to thwart thieves.

Sea Dog

A dog that drowned on the Tudor warship the *Mary Rose* went on to star at the 2011 Crufts dog show in London. The sea dog's skeleton was recovered when King Henry VIII's flagship (which sank in 1545) was raised from the seabed off England's South Coast. Its skeleton was found trapped in a doorway and re-assembled. After Crufts, it was displayed in a permanent spot in Portsmouth at the Mary Rose Museum.

Golden Mascot

A goldfish became one of the more unusual mascots for a professional football club in 2005. The lucky fish had been washed from its domestic bowl during floods in the northwest region of England and incredibly, was found alive on the waterlogged pitch of Carlisle United FC. Its rescuer was Emma Story, daughter of club chairman Fred, and she christened the fish Judy. As the struggling team won its next match, Judy came to epitomize the club's fighting spirit and was placed in a bowl in the reception area. The team rose three divisions over the next few years.

Leading From the Front

The Romans never left home without their canine warriors as they built a massive empire ranging from Asia to Britain. Each legion was assigned a whole company of dogs for hunting, seeking out the enemy and attack.

Horse is Cup Final Hero

A horse overshadowed 200,000 people when it became the hero of the 1923 football cup final in England. Bolton Wanderers and West Ham United qualified to play the first FA Cup final at the prestigious new 125,000-capacity Wembley Stadium and 200,000 fans tried to get in. Enter into the milling crush PC George Scorey and his white horse Billy of the London Metropolitan Police, who spent 45 minutes nudging the good-natured crowd back from the pitch so that the match could take place. The event, won 2-0 by Bolton, was named the "White Horse Final".

Conversations With Koko

Koko the gorilla proved apes can talk back... without uttering a single word. Born in San Francisco, USA, Koko began being taught American Sign Language by a scientist in 1972 and by 2000, she had a working vocabulary of 1,000 signs. With the ability to understand 2,000 words of English, she could argue, make jokes and even tell lies.

Girl Power

Although Flipper, the bottlenose dolphin of the films and TV series of the 1960s, was portrayed as a male, females played the star part. Suzy, Kathy, Patty, Scotty and Squirt all played Flipper because females are less aggressive and their skins less scarred from fighting. But there was one trick the girls couldn't master – the famous tail walk – for which a male dolphin named Clown was brought in.

Doggy Saviour

Rin Tin Tin saved many screen lives in a long film career and also reputedly saved a whole movie studio. The German shepherd dog's first starring role was alongside Claire Adams in *Where the North Begins* (1923). The film was such a huge success it has often been credited with saving the then-struggling Warner Brothers from bankruptcy.

Joining the Luftwoofer?

Adolf Hitler's Third Reich attempted to create a whole army of speaking dogs during World War II. German Army scientists at the training school in Leutenberg, near Hannover, researched trying to get dogs to read, talk and spell in a bid to win the war. The Nazi philosophy was that the bond between humans and dogs could be made so strong that the creatures could achieve much more and be capable of human traits.

Ancient Ally

One of the earliest recordings of dogs being used in combat was at the Battle of Marathon, between the Greeks and Persians in 490BC. A mural depicting the battle, in which the Greeks repelled the Persian invaders, celebrates a protection dog at the side of its master, engaging the invading Persians without hesitation.

On Guard

The guard-like qualities of the German shepherd meant that by the end of the Great War of 1918, there were more than 48,000 dogs in service with the German military who did not pay a pfennig for them. They were bred specifically for their guarding ability by Max von Stephanitz and offered free to the forces.

Treo the Hero

An army search dog was honoured with Britain's animal version of the Victoria Cross for saving soldiers' lives in Afghanistan in 2010. The black labrador Treo, from 104 Military Working Dog Support Unit in Rutland, was awarded the Dickin Medal by the veterinary charity, the People's Dispensary for Sick Animals (PDSA), after twice finding hidden bombs in Helmand Province.

Hot Dog

Nero the black labrador was rescued from a mountain, not because of exposure but because he was too hot. His owner rang the Mountain Rescue Service for Wales' Mount Snowdon in 2011 because the 30kg (66lb) dog was struggling in the heat. Three strong rescuers found the distressed creature and took it in turns to carry him down across their shoulders. Luckily, Nero quickly recovered the strength in his failing legs and his raw pads healed in no time at all.

Baywatch Bullock

As they swept into action, Baywatch-type rescuers might have expected Pamela Anderson but all they got was a panicked bullock. Lifeguards on jet skis rescued the runaway creature from the sea off Baggy Point, Devon in 2011. Frightened, like the rest of the herd by loud music from a nearby festival, he escaped from his field, crossed a busy road and jumped off a cliff into the sea. Thankfully, he was rescued wet but unhurt.

The Crate Escape

Pigs devised a co-ordinated escape plan from an abattoir in Novokuznetsk, Russia in 2011. After smelling blood, the team of eight pigs hurtled to one side of the trailer they were in, turned it over and managed to get away.

Chocolat's the Cream

In 2011, Chocolat the British Army dog became a hero among soldiers fighting in Afghanistan by not only sniffing out a Taliban bomb-making factory but also the booby traps that were protecting it. With a fine record for alerting troops to Improvised Explosive Devices (IEDs), Chocolat found the bomb plant in Helmand Province and also a safe way to get past a series of ingenious booby-traps that were potentially fatal.

Cheating Cheetahs

Predatory cheetahs can forget the pronghorn antelope as a meal option. While the cat is the fastest animal on earth at 100–105kph (62–65mph), it quickly runs out of steam. The pronghorn makes its escape at a steady 56kph (35mph) – but can keep it up for over 6km (4 miles).

Playing It Cool

Animals that often fall prey to hunting lions don't necessarily run away from them. They seem to know the fact that lions kill only when hungry. Scientists observed antelopes and zebras could usually sense if lions were out to kill and if not, will often ignore those wandering close to them.

Cliff, the Hero Dog

A dog's barking led to its injured owners being rescued from the bottom of a 70m (230ft) cliff. The Welsh springer spaniel led rescuers to the cliff edge in Devon, England in 2011 and then plunged 23m (75ft) over the edge to watch over her owners as a lifeboat rescued them.

Doggy Driver

A miniature poodle called Bubbles was taught by her owner to drive a children's electric car. She was often seen at the wheel on the pavements of Miami, Florida.

Deadly Package

A Swedish man tried to smuggle some of the deadliest snakes in the world – in his trousers! He was arrested in Australia in 2003 with the snakes, including four king cobras, strapped to his legs. The smuggler was extremely lucky as a bite from the fangs of a king cobra results in severe pain, blurred vision, vertigo, drowsiness and paralysis. Cardiovascular collapse leads to coma and death from respiratory failure.

Rinty the Trouper

Rin Tin Tin, star of many films of the early twentieth century, was once a shell-shocked victim of The Great War (1914–18). After being discovered in a bombed-out house in Lorraine, France in 1918, he was adopted by American serviceman Lee Duncan. He was named after the "good-luck" puppet French children gave to US soldiers and at the war's end Duncan took him back to his home in Los Angeles, California. Nicknamed "Rinty" by his owner, the dog learned tricks and could leap great heights. After being talent-spotted performing at a dog show, his big break came when he stepped in for a recalcitrant wolf.

Cat Goes Flying

Rocky the cat loved to play when annoying houseflies were about but in springing to catch one, he plummeted 30m (100ft) off the 11th-storey balcony of his owners' apartment in Lucerne, Switzerland. Amazingly, he survived and recovered from a broken leg and bruised liver.

Phantom Jump

A racehorse threw away one of the greatest races in the British racing calendar when it suddenly tried to jump a fence that wasn't there. Devon Loch was just 36m (40 yards) from victory in the 1956 Grand National and was smoothly on the run in when he mysteriously jumped into the air and belly-flopped. The horse, owned by Queen Elizabeth, the Queen Mother, was unable to continue and allowed its rival ESB to go on to win. Devon Loch went down in racing history as a failure, while his jockey Dick Francis became a bestselling crime novelist.

Naked Ape

Guru the chimpanzee puzzled scientists in 2011 because he was completely bald. He was taken to Mysore Zoo in southern India after being rescued from a circus, where his treatment appears to have led to the hair loss condition alopecia.

'Ear This

Hollywood makeup artists had their talents put to the test when preparing the star of the 1934 film, *The Mighty Barnum*, for the cameras. For a reason known only to themselves, the casting department selected Indian elephant Anna May for the role of circus owner P.T. Barnum's famous Jumbo. The only problem was that the original Jumbo was a larger African elephant, so the makeup people had to fit a huge pair of false ears and larger tusks over Anna May's smaller ones.

Oil Be Damned!

A budgerigar decided to take a bath in a deep-fat fryer at his home in Wootton Basset, England. After the 1996 incident he was rushed to a vet, who incubated him for 24 hours before his feathers were thoroughly cleaned of oil. Ironically, the budgie's name was Chips.

Bionic Cat

A pioneering (and world-first) operation gave prosthetic feet, and a new life, to Oscar the cat in 2011. His rear paws were chopped off when he was hit by a combine harvester the previous year near his home on the Channel Island of Jersey, but in the immortal words of *The Six Million Dollar Man* American TV series of the 1970s, surgeon Noel Fitzpatrick said: "We have the technology to rebuild him." The artificial feet were fixed to Oscar's anklebones by pegs coated with the special chemical hydroxyapatite which promoted bone growth and encouraged bone cells to bond with metal. Skin also regrew to seal the area against infection. Soon after his operation, Oscar was running and jumping about again as normal.

Junk Food

It is no myth that ostriches are prone to eating strange objects that attract them but a post-mortem on the stomach contents of one bird found coins, a gold necklace, a tyre valve, pencil, three feet of rope, a spoon, comb, clock key and a roll of camera film.

Whale Of a Thank You

There wasn't a dry eye to be seen when a whale said "thanks" to divers who had saved her life in 2008. Trapped in crab traps off the Farallon Islands of California, the female humpback faced certain death. Volunteer divers used knives to cut hundreds of rope strands from the whale and were rewarded by the sight of the creature swimming joyous circles in the Pacific Ocean. She then returned, nudging and pushing each diver individually in a tear-jerking expression of gratitude.

Net Favourite

Ariel the paralysed lion was one of the most popular animals on earth during 2011 with 35,000 Internet fans. A rare degenerative disease left him unable to walk but after his plight reached worldwide knowledge via the Facebook social networking site, his popularity soared from five in May 2011 to many thousands. Ariel, three, of São Paulo, Brazil also received thousands of pounds in donations toward the £7,000-a-month care bill ($11,000). The veterinary surgeon treating the big cat was hopeful that he would eventually recover from his illness.

Special Fur-ces

Austria introduced dogs into its elite forces in 2010, teaching them how to parachute and abseil. SAS-type troops leapt thousands of feet from aircraft and climbed steep precipices with dogs strapped to them.

Doggy Saviours

In an unlikely and unexpected alliance, Anatolian shepherd dogs have helped save the lives of wild cheetahs in Africa. The big guard dogs from Turkey were brought into farming areas of central, eastern and southwestern Africa from 1994 onwards to scare off hungry cheetahs who had acquired a taste for the relatively easy prey of cattle and goats. The dogs did such a good job that the number of cheetahs – a vulnerable species – being trapped or killed as pests dropped significantly.

Kiss of Life

A vet saved the life of a bald eagle with mouth-to-beak resuscitation. The injured bird was being operated on for shoulder and leg injuries when it suddenly stopped breathing. Jeff Cooney, a vet in Oregon, USA, breathed new life into Patriot the eagle and got his heart going again.

Loud Speaker

Stand back if you get into conversation with an African cicada as it produces the loudest call among insects – 106.7 decibels at a distance of 45cm (18in). That's almost as loud as being in the mosh pit of a rock concert! Long conversations are out, too, as cicadas live only 30–40 days.

Fossil Ousted

When you're all of 150 million years old, you don't expect to have to change species but it happened to Archaeopteryx in 2011. As one of the most precious and oldest fossils in the Natural History Museum in London's South Kensington, archaeopteryx was considered a bird because of its feathers. But the discovery of a 155 million-year-old Xiaotingia dinosaur fossil in China meant a rethink by paleontologists who decided Archaeopteryx is a dinosaur, too – albeit one in transition into the earliest of birds during the Jurassic period.

Adoring Adolf

During the 1930s a dog was taught by German Army scientists to say "Mein Führer" (my guide) when asked the question: "Who is Adolf Hitler?" At the time Hitler was the new Chancellor of Germany and leader of the Nazi Party and had styled himself "Führer" to his adoring public.

Ruff Ride

Donald the dog survived being stuck to the front of a car for 30 minutes as it sped along at 97kph (60mph). In 2011, the 14-year-old Jack Russell crossbreed was blown into the path of a car in Uttoxeter, Staffordshire in England. Believing he had hit a cardboard box, the motorist carried on driving for another 20 minutes before frantic barking alerted him. Firemen needed cutting equipment to extract the dog from the front of the car. An hour later, Donald was tucking into a hearty meal at home, with just a few scratches.

Cliff-plunge Survivor

Oscar the golden labrador survived a 60m (200ft) plunge down a cliff in 2011. It was a miraculous escape for the dog, which suffered just a broken leg after tumbling from a cliff path near Scarborough, Yorkshire in England. Ironically, his owner followed the dog seconds later (he was looking for Oscar, who was suddenly not at his heels, and also plunged over the edge to sustain a broken thigh and wrist). Fortunately, Oscar and his owner were airlifted to safety and recovered completely from their ordeal.

Flight Assistance

A bat survived several weeks trapped in a locked builder's hut in Somerset, England, in 2011. Staff from the Royal Society for the Prevention of Cruelty to Animals (RSPCA) rescued the half-starved bat and nursed it back to health and then helped it to fly again – something it had apparently forgotten how to do.

Shell-Shocked

An ostrich in China laid an egg weighing 2.3kg (5lb) in 1997, which could support the weight of a human. It was the equivalent of 24 hen's eggs. The average size of an ostrich egg is 1.4kg (3lb).

Terrapin Terror

A tiny terrapin escaped death under hundreds of feet when it was found on the platform of a busy London railway station. Amazingly, the reptile was spotted among the commuter crowds by two passengers who plucked it to safety and kept it in a bath at home until an animal protection society could collect it.

Eight Lives Left?

A kitten survived 45 days trapped in a container being shipped across the Pacific Ocean. The kitten weighed just 0.9kg (2lb) when the container was finally opened in Calgary, Canada after a 16,000km (10,000-mile) journey from China in 2010. Mandarin (as the cat was named by staff at the Calgary tiling firm where she was found) was thought to have lived on a few mice and condensation water.

Speeding Cat

Rastus the cat was capable of high speeds because he regularly toured New Zealand on owner Mark Corkhill's vintage motorcycle. The pair have notched up 240,000km (150,000 miles), with Rastus having his own scarf and miniature crash helmet.

Long-Lost Pal

Scruffy the toy poodle was reunited with his owner 549 days after going missing. He was found in the city of Oxford, England almost two years later and 160km (100 miles) away from his original home in Corringham, Essex. Scruffy was micro-chipped so it was still a joyous 47th birthday for his owner Julia Moran after being reunited with her pet.

Free-Fall Feline

Andy, a cat owned by Florida Senator Ken Myer, fell from the sixteenth floor (60m/200ft) of an apartment building but landed unharmed.

Mixed Marriage

A liger called Hercules was the accidental result of a secret love affair in 2007 between a male lion and a female tiger. The parents lived close together at the Institute of Greatly Endangered and Rare Species, in Miami, Florida. By the time he was three, he was a huge cat weighing half a tonne and standing 3m (10ft) tall on his hind legs.

Vital Birth

Having the largest recorded litter of six in captivity was of greater significance than tiger parents Betty and Conde could appreciate. Normally tiger litters average three but doubling that at Argentina's Buenos Aires Zoo in 2007 meant a significant increase to the world population of highly-endangered Bengal whites.

Clone Success

The endangered species of mouflon sheep received a major boost in 2001 when scientists successfully cloned them. At the time the wild population of mouflon was a precarious 1,000, spread across the three Mediterranean islands of Cyprus, Sardinia and Corsica.

Acquired Taste

The Chinese delicacy, bird's nest soup, is made from the homes of the Asian cave swiftlets. But the birds build their nests out of nothing but their own saliva.

Lick of Life

A dog saved the life of a World War I sailor… with the flick of her tongue. A half-collie called Lassie was owned by the landlord of the Pilot Boat pub in the coastal town of Lyme Regis, England. On New Year's Day of 1915, the Royal Navy battleship *Formidable* was torpedoed. A life raft was washed ashore and dead sailors' bodies were laid out on the pub table. Lassie began to lick one sailor's feet and someone noticed the man was reacting to it and so they revived him. Lassie inspired the eponymous films and TV series that have been so popular.

Grey Matter

The US Army coloured coded their pack mules to suit particular situations during World War II. Brown mules were the norm but when grey ones were imported into the war effort from Iran, the Americans thought them too conspicuous and so they used an early version of the hair colorant Grecian 2000 to darken them. When winter came, however, the mules stood out against the snowy background and so they had to let their root colour grow back.

Race Fur Freedom

With shades of the hit animated movie *Chicken Run*, a ferret with more than 400 "friends" on a social networking site staged a daring breakout in 2011. Mista the ferret was in show business as one of eight owned by entertainer Gordon Tyler, who escaped from his network of hutches. Mr Tyler said Mista, who has his own Facebook page, was the most streetwise of all and probably led his mates astray. Ironically, Mr Tyler's show was titled "The Great Escape".

Mane Deterrent

A garage owner in New Mexico, USA was so sick of criminals breaking in to steal tools and goods from his premises that he decided giving his dog a haircut was the best deterrent. After giving the dog a "lion" cut, leaving a mane around the head and a hairy tip to the tail, he put the word out that he had a "Mexican lion" that would attack anyone daring to break in or climb his fence. His idea worked because from a distance the dog's silhouette resembled a lion and the number of raids dropped.

Eye For a Crime

A trio of turkey vultures (named after famous detectives Sherlock Holmes, Miss Marple and Columbo) has been trained in Lower Saxony, Germany to find dead bodies. The birds' keen sense of smell has been harnessed to locate murder victims, particularly in areas of Walsrode that are difficult to search.

Have You Herd This One?

Cows provided the toughest audience ever for a British comedian who milked his jokes for all they were worth in 2011. Milton Jones, a popular radio and stand-up performer, tried his act out in front of a herd of cows to see if Friesian cattle have a funny bone. Cow expert Bruce Woodacre monitored the animals' reaction as part of a study he was carrying out. Although Jones said his material was new, the cows had one beef – they claimed they'd "herd" some of them before!

Born to Roam For Rome

The ancient Britons may not have welcomed the Roman invasion of their country from 55BC onward but they soon learned to cash in on it. What became the Province of Britannia was well known for exporting dogs to other parts of the Roman Empire. References to these dogs by writers of the time suggest British dogs were both fast and strong and useful in hunting and battle. It is thought they were the progenitor to today's English mastiff and bulldog.

What's In a Name?

The breed name of the German shepherd had to be changed to make them acceptable in Britain and the USA after World War I. British and American troops returning from the conflict started to bring the dogs home with them but the name "Alsatian" was quickly devised to rid them of their association with the German enemy of the 1914-18 war. It was more than 50 years, and another World War later, before the breed name reverted once more to German shepherd.

Chirps Cheer

In 2011 the feel-good value of birdsong was recognized by the Mayor of a Californian desert town: the sound of birds was to be broadcast through street loudspeakers because the town council believed birdsong would make residents happier.

Dogged By Success

One of the biggest novelty songs in pop history – "(How Much Is) That Doggie in the Window?" – was attributed with sparking an 8 per cent jump in Kennel Club registrations when Patti Page took it into the US Top 10 chart in 1953.

Pin-Up Bird

Vets had to use microsurgery to insert tiny metal pins to fix the broken leg of a baby kestrel in 2011. The bird, nicknamed "Tiggywinkles" by staff at a wildlife hospital at Aylesbury in England, was just a few weeks old when he fell from a tree.

Rat Windfall

For a prisoner in Romania, rats proved to be a real earner. Having to share his Bucharest cell with the rodents and cockroaches was ruled by a court to be an abuse of his human rights and he was subsequently awarded £13,000 ($20,000) in compensation.

I'll Be Blowed

Carthaginian military commander Hannibal emerged from his 280km (174 miles) trek with elephants across the Alps only to find that in the meantime, his enemies – the Romans – had devised a defence again war tuskers. At the ensuing Battle of Trebia in 218BC they blew trumpets, which panicked the elephants.

Tug of Love

Bella the labrador ended up at the centre of a court case in 2011. A couple went to litigation to get her back after they had allegedly given her away to their dogsitter because they couldn't cope with the lively chocolate-coloured bitch. They even hired a "pet detective" to snatch Bella back, but a judge ruled that she should go back to her sitter and awarded costs against the pair.

Hot-Dog Row

A German shepherd was used by vegans objecting to a stall selling sausages in Berlin, Germany as an enforcer. Police had to be called in 2011 when the vegans set the animal on sausage seller Hendrik Zeiler, who had refused to let the protesting vegans put anti-meat stickers on his stall.

Swell Move

An alpaca took to the waves in 2010 as the latest surfing protégé of Domingo Pianezzi. The animal called Pisco was the first recorded instance of an alpaca surfing. Pianezzi had for 10 years been training dogs to surf at San Bartolo Beach in Lima, Peru. Just in case of a wipeout, Pisco wore a life jacket.

Just Slipping Next Door

An orange corn snake had a s-s-s-s-surprise for retired social worker Dorothy Rose by popping out of a kitchen cupboard in 2011. The 70-year-old, who has never kept snakes herself, reckoned the 1m (3.3ft) long non-venomous corn snake had escaped from a pet lover near her home in Portsmouth, England.

Well Bee-haved

A bee swarm that took up residence in the Groom family home in Repton, England, was allowed to stay. The bee community flew in in early 2011 and made their home in a chimney, but proved perfect lodgers by not being a nuisance or stinging anyone. In fact, Julie Groom said the bees' presence had helped one of her two children conquer apiphobia – a fear of bees.

No Claims Bone-Us

Over-friendly St Bernard dog Arthur managed to crash a car. Excited by someone walking past the vehicle he was sitting in, the 92kg (203lb) dog jumped on the handbrake and sent his owner's car rolling backward into another one in Kent, England in 2009. His owner had to send Arthur's photograph to the insurance company because technically he was in charge of the vehicle at the time of the crash.

Fox's Starring Role

But for the English ban on hunting them with hounds, a member of the British royal family might have yelled "tally-ho!" and galloped after a fox. But all HRH Princess Anne could do in 2011 was watch after a fox appeared before 82,000 at an England v Scotland rugby union international at Twickenham. The invader scampered across the pitch an hour before kick-off, then reappeared just minutes before the start to cheers from the capacity crowd.

Marley's No Dope

Marley the police sniffer dog went on a pub-crawl with his handler and rooted out a host of drug users and dealers. The Greater Manchester Police dog (trained to sit beside suspects with drugs) visited 15 pubs in a weekend in 2011, which led to 12 people being detained. His biggest success was sniffing out a dealer who had 14 bags of cocaine on him. A subsequent search of the suspect's home turned up a cannabis farm with £50,000 ($80,000) of the drug.

Hen Pecked?

Scientists in the 1950s developed glasses to stop chickens pecking out each other's feathers. While they didn't aid eyesight, the mini "peck specs" acted as blinkers so that chickens were less likely to find another's feathers. Excessive pecking of others in a brood can lead to serious injury but unfortunately the chicken glasses didn't take off as a practical idea.

Barking Mad?

Barking dogs led to feuding neighbours in England racking up a legal bill of £400,000 ($633,000) between them. The dispute over the dogs and other complex issues lasted from 2007–11 when a judgment was made against the couple whose dog was causing the nuisance.

Goat in the Money

Sarah, a goat living in Kentucky, USA, was left $115,000 (£72,000) in the will of her former owner.

Buzzed By Buzzard

A furious buzzard, objecting to a man running through its woodland territory in South Wales, inflicted head injuries on jogger Alan Rosier in 2011 that required hospital treatment.

Flippin' Arrogant!

A penguin that became a British TV chat show star developed ideas above his station. Pringle, a king penguin, refused to travel to filming dates for *The Russell Harty Show* in the 1980s in a mere travelling crate but would happily hop onto the back seat of a chauffeur-driven limousine.

Speed Trap?

Megan Wheeldon turned the clock back more than a century to find a more environmentally friendly alternative to the bus to get to school in a rural English village: pony and trap. With her mother Tracey, they hitched pony Skippy to the cart and rode the 6km (4 mile) round trip to the school in Derbyshire, England, in 2011. Megan, 10, was a regular competitor in horse-driving competitions.

Cat's 999 Lives

Police dashed to a London home after receiving two 999 emergency calls from the same number. Fearing the worst, they broke in to find the owners safe in their beds – but Chippa their cat was found walking on the buttons of the telephone, having repeatedly found the 9 and redial buttons!

Master Mess-Up

A brave dog's attempt to apprehend a sneak thief was foiled...
by its owner. In the 1909 incident, reported in *The New York
Times*, the dog successfully apprehended the thief, who had
been raiding the home of a Methodist minister in Bayonne, New
York, and held him. But the Revd. George Whitehead tried to
join in and in the resulting mêlée, the three became entangled,
allowing the thief to make good his escape.

Football Wedding Winger

A natty piece of wing play was a feature of the 2009 wedding of
Manchester United and England footballer Wes Brown to fiancée
Leanne Wassell. In a scene straight out of a Harry Potter film, an
owl delivered the couple's rings to the ceremony. Ollie the barn
owl swooped over guests bearing the rings in a velvet pouch. The
ceremony was at the aptly-named Peckforton Castle in Cheshire.

Doggy Diet

Stuffed toys, shoes, hairdryer parts and a watchstrap were
among items consumed by a pet dog belonging to British
novelist Jilly Cooper.

Having a Ball

A golf club employed Maudie the labrador to make full use
of her exceptional retrieval skills in finding lost balls. Paid 30p
(50 cents) a ball, in her career Maudie found more than 1,000
balls, including buried ones, at the Pyecombe course in West
Sussex, England.

Manager In the Doghouse

The dog of one of the world's top soccer managers fell foul of British law in 2007. José Mourinho, who had led Porto, Chelsea, Inter Milan and Real Madrid to success, was forced to race from an awards ceremony to save his Yorkshire terrier from arrest. He was responding to a panic call from his wife Tami after police had raided their London home looking for a dog allegedly in violation of Britain's strict quarantine regulations. The volatile Portuguese manager was arrested for obstruction, although no charges were filed. In the meantime, the fugitive Yorkie bitch Leya disappeared only to resurface with relatives in his native Portugal.

Getting Waspish

Soccer players demanded a change of shirt after many of their Abingdon United team were stung by wasps during the 2003 season. They claimed their bright yellow strip was attracting the insects.

Snappy Gear

Giant crocodiles were fitted with satellite navigation tags in 2011 to prevent their toll on villagers on the island of Borneo. Three people a year had been eaten by the crocs, which grow to up 3m (10ft) in length, so British scientists devised the Sat-Nav idea, each device costing £1,500 ($2400), so they could alert villagers if the reptiles leave their river home and head their way.

Harassed by a Hawk

Canada's Toronto Football Club brought in a Harris hawk called Bitchy in 2007 to help keep its stadium clear of seagulls. The birds were attracted from nearby Lake Ontario and had been enjoying a good free meal amid the post-match litter.

Heavy Metal Dog

Labradors are renowned for their capacity to eat almost anything but a 25cm (10in) monkey wrench surprised even hardened veterinarians. Lattie was taken to a Massachusetts vet because she was, most unusually, off her food. An X-ray and an operation revealed the tool, which, incredibly, had been eaten a month earlier.

Massive Mastiff Litter

Tia the mastiff claimed a new world record in 2005 for giving birth to the most puppies in one litter – 24. Although four of the puppies did not survive, the bitch from Cambridgeshire, England also claimed the record for the most surviving puppies.

TV Addict

A Chinese family always had a guest when they settled down to watch TV – an owl. Initially, the bird flew into the Jiangxi province home of farmer Zhang Liuyou in 1992 attracted by the light from the screen. The owl became addicted to the action on screen and returned every night for years, settling on a roof beam or the table to watch. As soon as the TV was switched off, the owl took to his wings for a night's hunting.

Bee-spoke Suits

China staged a bee-attracting competition in 2011. Contestants, all beekeepers, dressed in just shorts and goggles, stood on scales with a special queen bee and did their best to attract the most bees to settle on their bodies. The winner at the Hunan province contest was Wang Dalin, who was smothered in 26kg (57lb) of bees – 3kg (7lb) more than his nearest rival.

Kit-Katfish

Gary the gourami had to go cold turkey to get over a chocolate addition. Staff at London's Sea Life Aquarium in 2011 were mystified when Gary, who had been donated and weighed in at 3.9kg (8.5lb), would not eat the traditional food he would find in his Asian home waters. A call to his previous owners revealed why he was so faddy and had outgrown his previous tank: he was fed a diet of Kit Kat chocolate-covered wafer confectionery. Gary, thought to be 10 at the time and 40cm (16in) in length had to be served crushed Kit Kat inside grapes and bananas to tempt him back to a normal diet.

Grass Roots Approach

Sheep, goats and chickens made sure the Ipswich Town professional football team had one of the best-mown and greenest grass pitches to play on during the 1920s. The groundsman of the time, Walter Woollard, kept a variety of herbivores to crop, manure and aerate the English club's ground.

Roo-ing the Day

An unprovoked attack by escaped kangaroo Eddie was the morning surprise for Phyllis Johnson as she hung out the washing in Queensland, Australia. The furious roo, on the run from a wildlife centre, ripped down her laundry and mugged her in 2011. Police used pepper spray to calm the kangaroo and Mrs Johnson needed minor hospital treatment.

Weighty Problem

An orangutan had to go on a lifesaving diet after being adopted by the Monkey World Sanctuary in England, in 2011. Oshine weighed a massive 95kg (210lb) – twice her natural weight – when she arrived from South Africa, where she had been indulged with sweets and jelly. A healthy diet quickly reduced her bodyweight by 20 per cent.

24-Carrot Champ

Ralph, a Continental Giant rabbit, claimed the new world record for being the biggest rabbit in 2011. One-year-old Ralph, who was1.2m (4ft) long, weighed 19.5kg (43lb) – more than an average three-year-old child. Owner Pauline Grant of Uckfield, East Sussex in England relied on handouts from kind neighbours to feed Ralph, who had already become too heavy for her to lift.

Long-Distance Love

Love just wasn't around the corner for Jasmina the red panda – it was 18,870km (11,725 miles) away. Breeding the rare animal from Bristol Zoo in England meant going the extra mile – well, 11,725 miles actually – to Wellington, New Zealand. Panda stud "Sir Ed" was shipped in from the southern hemisphere in 2011 because red pandas are a threatened species and it was essential to boost numbers.

Spider Outshines Shuttle

Even spiders like their few minutes of fame but in the case of one, it was 26 seconds. An inquisitive arachnid crawled onto NASA's launch camera at Cape Canaveral in Florida as it recorded a launch of the space shuttle Atlantis in 2007. The magnified insect could be seen online appearing to take a bite out of the shuttle's nose cone. Satisfied with its worldwide fame, the spider simply hopped off!

Firefighting Elephants

In 2012, elephants and rhinoceros were being considered for a move of 10,240km (6,363 miles) to carry out fire prevention duties. The African natives could be introduced to northern Australia to prevent bushfires because they would contain the spread of invasive fire-fuelling grass, an Australian scientist had proposed. The "grass-eating machines" could limit the damage from the continent's rampant bushfires, one of which in 2011 covered a 64,519 sq km (24,911 sq mile) area of the Outback in central Australia.

Millionaire Pooch

A dog costing hundreds of thousands of pounds made a VIP entrance at its new home in northern China. The rare black Tibetan mastiff cost a millionaire woman, identified only as "Wang", four million yuan ($600,000). The dog was met at Xi'an Airport by a convoy of 30 Mercedes-Benz luxury cars and a banner of welcome. Wang said she had spent a great deal of time searching for a genuine Tibetan mastiff.

Whale of a Voice

Jet engines pall when a blue whale starts talking. Its mammoth moans in communication with others of its kind are not diminished by water and have been measured at 188 decibels – 68dB more than a military jet engine!

Feeling Sheepish

A sheep ended up on a boozy night out with four top British footballers in 2007. The creature was "sheep-napped" when the four unidentified players were taking a minibus home after their night out in Wales. For reasons known to themselves they stopped and bundled the surprised sheep into the vehicle – and promptly forgot all about it! Next morning they panicked when they found it still in the van and released her in the first field they came to.

Jumbo Night Out

No bottle of rum was safe when a herd of binge-drinking elephants was about in Bengal during the 1980s. They particularly targeted an army base where rum was stored and they would crash their way in, then break the necks off bottles and swig the contents before going on a drunken rampage of destruction. They were so addicted that in their haste to get drunk, they braved electrified fences and fires designed to scare them.

Taking Life Slowly

A tortoise lived so long it spanned from the age of voyages by sailing ship to Australia to jet travel. Explorer Captain Cook presented the tortoise named Tui Malila to the Tonga royal family in the 1770s and it lived a well-fed and comfortable record lifespan of 188 years. Dying in 1965, the tortoise lived through a period of history that saw Napoleon come and go; two World Wars, the Nuclear Age and the Swinging Sixties.

Long In the Tooth

A killer whale outlived many of the folk who used to see him make annual winter visits to Twofold Bay in the Australian state of New South Wales. "Old Tom", who was especially distinguishable by a special pattern and an unusually shaped dorsal fin, was reported as being seen every year from 1843 to 1930, giving him a record age for his species.

Dangerous Neighbours

An alligator, cobra, puff adder and a rattlesnake were seized when health officials raided a small apartment in Boca Raton, Florida in 2012.

For the High Jump

The world frog leap record was set in California, USA in 1986. A high-kicking lady by the name of Rosie the Ribeter jumped a length of 6.5m (21.3ft).

Gander's Revenge

Disturbing the nesting idyll of a pair of Canada geese in England came back to haunt a former dentist and left him seriously injured. Previous visits past the Sussex nest on his quad bike were greeted by a series of flapping wings and hissing, but the next time a vengeful gander really hit back. As Jan Pieniazek, 64, passed the nesting site on a lake bordering his smallholding, the angry gander crashed onto his head. Jan lost control of his bike and collided with a tree, suffering an open fracture of his leg. Hearing his frantic cries for help, a neighbour called the emergency services.

Government Rat

A rat problem for Britain's Prime Minister David Cameron got an unexpected airing in front of millions of TV viewers. As the BBC's political correspondent Gary O'Donoghue broadcast from in front of the famous black door of 10 Downing Street in 2011, a rat made an unscheduled dash across the screen, highlighting the problem at the PM's residence.

Long-Legged Vandal

Ozzy the ostrich lived up to his namesake by going on the rampage in Poland. Police in the city of Poznan were inundated with calls about what was thought to be a gang of vandals in action during the night. Racing to the scene, they found 1.8m (6ft) tall Ozzy attacking a barbecue, having already smashed down a fence. Ozzy, a pet named after hell-raising Black Sabbath singer Ozzy Osbourne, was "arrested" and taken to a safari park to cool off.

Oh, Deer!

Bulls in china shops are nothing compared to a disoriented deer that mistakenly entered a fruit and vegetable shop in England in 2011. The creature, previously seen paddling in the sea at Dawlish in Devon, ran into the back office of the shop and in its panic, caused havoc by scattering papers and knocking over furniture.

Dog Ends Career

The professional career of goalkeeper Chic Brodie was brought to an untimely end by a dog. During a game between Brodie's team Brentford and Colchester United in November 1970, a black-and-white terrier invaded the field and tore about, upending players and linesmen alike, but the referee refused to stop the match. The mutt then decided to chase a back pass from Brentford's centre-half Peter Gelson to his goalie. Keeping his eye firmly on the ball, Brodie bent down to scoop it up but the energetic pooch leapt at the keeper and sent him crashing. In a bizarre twist of fate, Brodie's kneecap was shattered in the incident and he never played professionally again.

Dog Walking Into Trouble

Football star Carlo Cudicini ended up undergoing an operation after he suffered an injury while out walking his dog in London.

Nostril Hideaway

Scientists added a new species to the list of life on earth in 2010 after looking up someone's nose. The tyrant king leech (Tyrannobdella rex) was officially classified after it was found living in the nasal membrane of someone in Peru. It was given its fearsome name because of its oversized jaws.

I'll Be Blowed

When you are a retriever dog, you retrieve things and bring them right back to your owner – even a live hand grenade! And that's exactly what a golden retriever did while out walking in Vienna, Austria. The dog terrified its owner Julia Meye by picking up an old hand grenade, presumably left over from World War Two, and dropping it right at her feet. Julia quickly put some distance between herself and the dog's dangerous "find" – and left the Bomb Disposal Squad to deal with it.

Rule of Thumb

Thumbelina went into the records books in 2006 as the world's smallest horse at just 43cm (17in) tall. Indeed, she was barely larger than a domestic cat. Thumbelina was born on a farm in St Louis, Missouri, where Paul and Kay Goessling bred miniature horses but she was tiny even when compared to the couple's other horses, who typically reach about 86cm (34in).

Ear, Look at This!

Doctors were in for a surprise when they examined a patient who complained of pain and itching in her ears. They found a colony of ants living in the ears of a 16-year-old girl in Taiwan, with more than 20 insects nesting in the right ear alone. The cause of the infestation was the girl's love of snacking in bed, which attracted the ants who decided her ears were a warm place to nest. Doctors removed the ants and told the teenager to stop snacking in the wee small hours.

Russian Idea Gets Tanked

The best-laid plans of men can be thwarted if they mess with dogs. During World War Two, the Soviet Union came up with the idea of "anti-tank dogs". The plan was for dogs with bombs strapped to their backs to be trained to run toward enemy tanks and to detonate the explosives upon impact. But the dogs were having none of this suicidal plan and managed to foil it in a mercifully short time because they couldn't distinguish between Russian and enemy tanks. Also, when they got frightened or confused they ran back to their handlers – with the explosive still intact!

Let Sleeping Snakes Lie

A viper, which had found an ideal sleeping place in a frying pan, objected to being disturbed and bit a Croatian housewife on the arm. The life of the woman, from the town of Sucurje, was saved by an antidote jab which counteracted the poisoning.

Going Bananas

An escaped chimpanzee trashed the car of a policeman who tried to apprehend her. Furious Sueko, who weighed in at 136kg (300lb) damaged the car's bodywork and windows after being confronted by police in Kansas City, USA. She was pacified with a dart from a tranquilizer gun, confiscated from her private owners and placed in a zoo.

Fatal Squeeze

An over-affectionate boa constrictor killed its owner by squeezing just a little bit too hard. In 2011, the 3m-long (10ft) reptile became the first boa constrictor to kill a person in the US. The red-tailed boa wrapped itself around the shoulders and neck of its owner then strangled him as he showed his pet to a friend. Eyewitnesses defended the snake saying this was not a deliberate attack.

Stupidly Brave

A dog named Stupid must have been due for a name change in 1996 after taking on the powerful jaws and razor-sharp teeth of a crocodile. His bravery on a riverbank near Cairns, Australia saved the life of owner and fisherman Robert Moodie. He was trying to retrieve a lost lure in the murky waters when a huge crocodile struck. With Robert unconscious and in danger of being dragged away as a croc meal, Stupid confronted the reptile and scared it away.

Croc-ked Plane

In a scene that might have come straight from a Hollywood movie, a crocodile smuggled aboard an aeroplane caused a crash that killed 20 people in 2011. After escaping from its bag, it sent the panic-stricken crew and passengers rushing to the nose end of the airliner flying over the Republic of Congo. Their combined weight fatally affected the plane's equilibrium and it crashed into a house. Ironically, only the croc survived the crash.

Bald Fury

Furious American bald eagles reacted to their nesting idyll being disturbed by attacking people who were going to the post office in Dutch Harbour, Alaska. The aerial marauders dive-bombed what they saw as "intruders" and drew blood on several occasions.

Fox Flap

Urban foxes showed their cunning by repeatedly getting into a London house – via a cat flap! In 2011, a student had to be treated after being nibbled by a fox while asleep and two years earlier, a fox had got in to another bedroom and ripped up clothes.

Cow With a Beef

A runaway cow brought parts of an English road to a standstill as emergency services battled for seven hours to recapture it in 2011. Dozens of police crews and a helicopter followed as the cow evaded capture in Hull, causing mainline rail services to be suspended for a while.

Cat Rap

Max the cat took the blame for his owner being arrested on suspicion of drink driving in England in 2010. All Max did – while his owner, professional cricketer Graeme Swann, was celebrating his 31st birthday with friends – was to investigate under the floorboards and get stuck. Swann, alerted to the cat's plight by wife Sarah, decided to drive at 3 a.m. to get screwdrivers from a supermarket in West Bridgford, England instead of walking the 10-minute trip. Swann, an England international bowler, was stopped by police on the way and charged, but later escaped conviction on a technicality.

Criminal Tail

A squirrel's face was circulated on wanted posters in Rheine, Germany after it went on the rampage in a furniture store. The animal triggered alarms after breaking into the shop and was captured on CCTV cameras as it leapt about and destroyed sheets and curtains. No "arrest" was made, however!

Wrong Chord

Heavy metal wasn't music to the ears of a pack of wolves in Norway, in 2011. The snarling creatures were sent packing by schoolboy Walter Eikrem, 13, after he played "Overcome" by American heavy metal band Creed at them on his cell phone. The wolves were threatening the boy as he walked home from school at Rakkestad and ran off, baffled, when he turned his phone (playing Creed) toward them at full volume. Perhaps they might have preferred 1970s band Steppenwolf?

Führer Fury

A dog who learned to give a Nazi salute caused a row in Germany in 2011. It was trained to raise its right paw in salute for a TV drama about the *Hindenburg* airship disaster of 1937, but protesters claimed this was not politically correct. Animal trainer Hannes Jaenicke rejected the criticism, saying dogs in show business were professionals just like any other actor and had to play difficult roles.

Plane Pain

A stowaway scorpion stung a passenger on a journey from Seattle to Anchorage, Alaska in the USA. Jeff Ellis, 55, woke up on the Alaska Airlines' flight to find the scorpion on his arm but, not realizing what it was, he brushed it off only for the creature to return and sting his elbow. Ellis coolly grabbed the poisonous insect and handed it to a flight attendant to get rid of it. Apart from a raised heart rate, he was unaffected by the sting when examined by a doctor but was later offered two round-trip tickets, as well as 4,000 "Frequent Flier" miles in compensation. Alaska Airlines said that it had never had scorpions on its flights before and believed the scorpion had boarded when the aircraft had been operating a route to Austin, Texas.

Dolphin Security Guards

The US Navy employed underwater friends to stop sabotage attacks on ships during the Vietnam War of the 1960s and 70s. Dolphins were trained to emit a shrill noise if human intruders were detected swimming toward the naval base at Cam Ranh Bay.

Player Gets Antsy

Furious ants interrupted a football match in Brazil in 2008. It started when Marcos Paulo stunned the watching crowd by suddenly sprinting off the field and straight into the dressing room. The Santacruzense player had been rolling around on the pitch in order to gain a free kick for a foul but in the process disturbed an ants' nest and within seconds, his chest, sides and legs were a swarming black mass of angry insects. The referee, misunderstanding his predicament, tried to book the player, who first rolled in a puddle and then sprinted for the showers to wash away the mass of frenzied biting ants.

Feeling Sheepish

In 2012, a video of sheep running rings round a car in Russia soon became an internet favourite. Hundreds of thousands of people worldwide watched the 22-second clip, shot on a camera phone, fascinated as a driver was surrounded by an unrelenting torrent of sheep. The car crept forward, beeping its horn and despite revving of the engine, the persistent sheep continued their frenzied loop round the vehicle.

Has Nessy Moved?

One of the animal mysteries of 2012 was the video footage of a sea monster that looked very much like Scotland's legendary Loch Ness monster. But the new one was filmed in Bristol Bay, Alaska. With a horse-like head, a long neck, big eyes and humps on its back, it undulated above the surface for just a moment before diving back underwater – leaving seasoned sailors scratching their heads.

Loose Moose Incident

A wandering moose interrupted the burgeoning international career of Norwegian footballer Svein Grondalen in 1974. The defender, who had a reputation for a robust style of play, was in a forest on a training run when he collided with a moose. These creatures can weigh up to 550-700kg (1,200-1,500lb) and have a body length of 2.5m (8ft). The player, who was just establishing himself in his national side, proved no match for the moose and sustained injuries that were bad enough to prevent him from playing for a while.

Fangs a Lot!

In 2012, a grateful white shark created a difficulty for the fisherman who saved her life. For two years, the 5m (16ft) giant of the seas just followed Australian Arnold Pointer's boat everywhere he went, which for a professional fisherman is a real problem because "Cindy", as he had christened her, scared all the fish away. Arnold saved the shark from certain death when he cut her free after being trapped in his nets. She turned on her back and let him stroke her belly and neck.

Nice to Meat You

Full-grown tigers wander happily among tourists at Thailand's Wat Pha Luang At Bua temple in Thailand. Tourists may pet them because the tigers are tamed by being fed with cooked meat, which does not give them a taste for blood.

Pickles is World Champ!

A mongrel dog called Pickles was the true hero of England winning the football World Cup in 1966. The 55cm (22in) Jules Rimet Trophy was stolen soon after arriving in England and the police were unsuccessful in getting it back until Pickles sniffed it out near his owner's London home. In fact, the theft was part of a ransom plot for which a gang was demanding £15,000 ($24,000) for the trophy's return. A man was later jailed and, ironically, the trophy was destined to remain in England for at least the next four years because Bobby Moore captained his country to a World Cup victory that has proved the only one for Engalnd so far.

Just a Wind-up

There was nothing paw about Striker the Border collie's feat in 2003. He claimed the record for the fastest car window opening by a dog when, using only his paw and nose, he unwound a non-electric window in just 13 seconds.

Killer Snail

A road crash in England was blamed on a snail, or possibly a slug. The creature made its way into a traffic light and caused a malfunction. This led to a head-on crash between cars at a single-lane bridge in Alvecote, West Midlands.

Elephant Executioners

Death by elephant was a common method of capital punishment in South and Southeast Asia until about 300 years ago. Elephants were trained to crush, dismember, or torture captives in public executions. They were able to kill their victims quickly or torture them slowly over a prolonged period. The practice, which went back thousands of years, has been recorded in numerous contemporary journals and accounts of life in Asia. Eventually it was suppressed after the European empires colonized the region.

F-owl Play

The death of a barn owl led to threats against a Colombian football league player in 2011. After being hit by the ball, the bird mascot of Junior Barranquilla football club lay stunned on the field of play. An opposing player – Luis Moreno of Deportivo Pereira – lashed out at it, booting it 3m (10ft) off the field. The owl died and as fans chanted "murderer" at the offending player, he needed a heavy guard to get out of the ground. He later apologized, claiming he wanted to see if the owl could fly.

Bird Strike

A swallow-like bird brought the Wimbledon tennis championships to a temporary halt in 2007 when it was killed in a mid-air collision with a 70mph shot from one of the players. A packed audience witnessed the bird's demise during a men's doubles match and millions more have since seen it on TV and the Internet as the unlikely tragedy played out.

Pet Hate

Even a spider can affect the world of football, it seems. Kaizer Chiefs and South African international goalkeeper Rowen Fernandez had to withdraw from a game after being bitten on one finger by his pet arachnid in 2003. Fernandez, nicknamed "Spider" for his love of the insects (as well as snakes), ended up in hospital but recovered after treatment and was soon back in the team.

Keeping Track

A ferret was rescued from a Scottish railway station after taking a train from England in 2011. The male ferret, named Mickey by animal welfare officers who took him in, was found at Edinburgh's Haymarket station after arriving on the cross-border train from London, almost 650km (400 miles) away.

You've Got Butterfly Mail

Hisayoshi Kojima was given 21 months in a Japanese prison for importing endangered butterflies by post. Instead of using the most common smuggling method – by air – he mailed them! Among the postings were two Queen Alexandra's birdwings, the world's largest butterfly.

Animal Lover Sheik

Animal-loving Saudi Sheik Mohammed al-Fassi put his wealth to work for stray cats. Appalled that so many of them were being destroyed, he set up a sanctuary in Florida, USA to house 100 cats.

Seagull's Fatal Flight

One of the more bizarre mementoes in any football club's trophy cabinet is a stuffed seagull in The Netherlands. Thousands of fans were in the Feyenoord Stadium in Rotterdam to witness the bird's untimely death in 1970, when a goalkeeper's kick blasted it out of the sky. Home keeper Eddie Treytel was the man who entered football folklore with a high kick upfield in a match against Sparta Rotterdam, which shot down the bird. Its body was retrieved, whisked off to a taxidermist and it has stood in pride of place beside Feyenoord's array of domestic and European trophies ever since.

Collaring Accolades

Priscilla the pig became a famous personality in 1984 because she saved a boy from drowning. The unlikely heroine heard the desperate cries of an 11-year-old boy, who had got out of his depth in Lake Somerville, near Houston, Texas. Despite being used only to paddling in water, Priscilla swam strongly to the middle of the lake and grabbed Anthony Melton by his collar, towing him to safety. She won a bravery award and the city of Houston declared a day of festivities in her honour.

Pants Hiding Place

A German reptile collector was jailed in 2008 after being caught cruelly trying to smuggle 44 geckos and skinks out of New Zealand concealed in a hand-sewn pouch in his underwear.

Oyster's Lip Service

An oyster became a star attraction in 1840s London because it could whistle. Discovered when a strange sound came from a barrel of oysters at a fishmonger's shop, the whistling saved the bivalve's life. Crowds went to hear the oyster, which was given the name of Molly by the shopkeeper, who refused offers from circus owners and theatre managers prepared to shell out for the phenomenon.

Snake in a Spin

A hissing sound really bothered a driver as he travelled through Switzerland. The noise seemed to be a puncture and so he stopped to change a wheel, but one look had him screaming and running away. A 1.2m (3ft 11¼in) viper was coiled up inside the wheel! The snake with its head in a spin was safely re-homed at a zoo by St Gallen police, who were called to the scene by the panicked driver.

Panda Love

A whole village was mobilized when a rare panda fell through ice in a remote part of China in 1994. Despite it being a dangerous wild animal, three brave young women risked their lives to dive in and rescue the bear. Once on the riverbank, the rest of the village rallied round and lit a fire to dry the panda. They also fed it a huge meal of bamboo, meat and sugar before it strolled back into the woods.

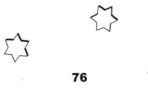

Star Traveller

A cat that disappeared for 16 months was found more than 480km
(300 miles) away after a journey that included a sea crossing.
In October 2009, Star went missing from her home on the Isle
of Wight on England's south coast and must have stowed away
for an hour's ferry ride to the mainland and kept moving north.
Star was identified by her microchip in York by a cats' protection
organization in February 2011 after covering almost 300 miles,
then reunited with her relieved owner, Harriet Parkinson.

Tortoise Takeout

Progress may have been slow but an abducted tortoise called Toffee
eventually found her way back home. It took the tortoise five weeks
to arrive across the road from her home on the Isle of Wight, England
after being carried off by a crow in 2011. Toffee was unharmed after
her ordeal and somehow had a homing instinct that enabled her to
arrive home after circumventing obstacles such as high walls.

Oops, Wrong Way!

An emperor penguin, which lost its bearings, was found
3,200km (2,000 miles) from its natural home in Antarctica.
The bird, which exists nowhere else other than the Antarctic,
was found on a beach on New Zealand's North Island, having
swum right past the South Island. But its problems in 2011
didn't end there: it had to be treated for a disease picked up in
the warmer waters of the Southern Ocean and then it made itself
ill by eating sand, which it mistook for the snow, of which it
devours a great deal in its natural environment. Wildlife officials
relocated the traveller as soon as it had recovered.

Tasmanian Devil

A cat raised eyebrows in Australia by disappearing from his home and turning up, three years and almost 4,000km later. Clyde the long-haired Himalayan went missing from the island of Tasmania, off South Australia. He made his way into the Outback and was identified via his electronic chip in Queensland, some 3,862km (2,400 miles) from home in 2011.

Life In the Fast Lane

A dog that escaped from a car at an Austrian service station caused major traffic jams as he ran along a motorway lane. The German shepherd blocked the A14 Inntal highway in 2011 as he evaded pursuing police. He was eventually captured after 4km (2.5 miles).

Iggy Pops Off

A Chocolate labrador called Iggy simply melted away when he was just 18 months old and stayed away – for five years! He was found as a stray and identified by his microchip some 210km (130 miles) from his home in Lancashire, England. In 2011, he was reunited with owner Brierley Howard, aged 12. The seven-year-old had been heartbroken at the loss of her beloved pet. But Iggy was in for surprise when he arrived back at his old home: a canine playmate called Odie had joined the Howard family during Iggy's long absence.

Hitting the Heights

Ham the Astrochimp went from obscurity in the forests of Cameroon to the stars in the 1960s. On January 31, 1961, he was secured in a Project Mercury space capsule and launched from Cape Canaveral, Florida, on a suborbital flight. The capsule suffered a partial loss of pressure during the flight, but Ham's space suit prevented him from suffering any harm. His lever-pushing skills during the 16min, 39s flight were only a fraction of a second slower than on Earth, proving that tasks could be performed in space. Ham splashed down in the Atlantic Ocean with a bruised nose, then lived for 17 years in zoos before his death at the age of 26 in 1983. Officially, he was known as "No. 65" before his flight and only named after a successful return to Earth. This was reportedly because officials did not want the bad press that would come from the death of a "named" animal, had the mission failed.

French Cat-astrophe

Sandy the cat was a truly loved pet and to prove it, owner Wendy Wilson made a 2,575km (1,600 miles) mercy dash to save her. Wendy had been feeding Sandy, who had been abandoned and turned up at her holiday home in Cruzy, Southern France, but she was actually at her English home in Suffolk when she heard that the cat was stuck on the roof of the French property. She made the trip back to France to help coax the stranded Sandy to safety.

Black Hills Exile

A mountain lion found dead after being hit by a vehicle in Connecticut, USA, in 2011, was a long way from home. DNA checks on the puma showed that it was from the Black Hills region of South Dakota, a trek of more than 3,200km (2,000 miles).

Van Cat

Snowy the cat went travelling in the back of a builder's van and was missing from his home near Swindon, England for more than a month. He was found 164km (102 miles) – and several counties – away in Bognor Regis, Sussex, and reunited with his owner, who was traced through a microchip implant.

Run, Rabbit, Run

A rabbit which stopped the game by dashing onto the pitch at Real Madrid's Bernabéu stadium during the 1996–97 season had a surprise coming. Real's super-fast defender Carlos Secretario sprinted after it – and caught it.

Kitty Nicker

Peter Weismantel feared he might get a bad reputation because of the number of pairs of stolen underwear that were building up in his home and so he grassed up the culprit – his cat Oscar. The 13-year-old was bringing home up to 10 items a night, so Peter (of Southampton, England) went to the police in 2010 to explain his innocence.

Flying Crimebusters

The most colourful rainforest birds in the world uncovered a wildlife smuggling operation. As they were being brought in to the USA in luggage, four birds of paradise escaped and flew around the heads of customs officials, alerting them to the crime in progress. With his cover obviously blown, the smuggler admitted also having monkeys concealed in his pants and illegally imported orchids elsewhere in his luggage.

A (Slow) Dash for Freedom

In 2010, Jamie the tortoise won the nickname of Houdini after successfully escaping from his home in Lincolnshire, England 50 times in 34 years. The unrepentant escape artist had spent around 130 days on the run since he was born. His longest spell away was three weeks during which he crossed a major road, unscathed.

Nose For the Job

A Doberman police tracker dog was a match for a criminal on the run in South Africa in 1925. Sauer, who was once considered unfit for police work, tracked his way into history when he followed the trail of a thief, without stopping, for 160 hot, gruelling kilometres (100 miles) across the barren and rocky Great Karoo region – and caught his man.

Bad Habits For Cheeta

Cheeta, the best-known chimpanzee in Hollywood movie history, developed a love of Cuban cigars and beers after becoming a box-office hit on Tarzan movies during the 1930s. He retired in 1948, but lived on to 80, a world record for a chimp in captivity.

Hardly a Cat-astrophe!

A cat called Charlie Chan received $250,000 (£157,000) from the will of an American surgeon in the 1960s, but was shortchanged because two other cats with whom he shared the house received $415,000 (£260,000).

Vocal Vocation

A verbose budgerigar became a TV and recording star because of his incredible talent for words. Every day of the eight years of his life he was taught a few new words and in nine months accrued a vocabulary of 300. By the time of his death in 1962, Sparkie, who was owned by an English teacher in Newcastle upon Tyne, England, had mastered 531 words, 383 sentences and eight nursery rhymes. Under the stage name of "Mr Chatterbox", he made several TV birdseed commercials and a record that taught owners how to teach their birds to talk. Urban myth it might be, but it is claimed his dying words were: "I love you, Mamma".

Dog's Extra Bite

A vet examining an under-the-weather dog in the USA found that he had more teeth that he should have. In 2011, an X-ray revealed the hound had swallowed his owner's false teeth and an operation was needed to remove them. We're not sure how keen the owner was to put them back in his own mouth, though!

Shark is Wartime 007

A shark was an unwitting ally to the British during the American War of Independence in the late 1770s. The American rebel ship Nancy was captured by the British Navy and, in his panic not to be unmasked as a blockage runner, the captain threw his ship's papers overboard and claimed to be Dutch. Enter a hungry and unsuspecting shark who scoffed the papers. In an amazing coincidence, the large shark was caught by another British ship a day later and the undigested – and guilt-proving – papers were retrieved.

Marmoset In a Hat

A passenger with a moving hat caused a stir on a 2010 flight from Peru to New York. First, his hat moved and then a marmoset – a small monkey – began climbing down the passenger's ponytail from its hiding place to spend the rest of the long flight obediently sitting on the man's seat.

Hippo Hooray!

Bookies might have given odds on the shark but a hippopotamus got the better of a very rare animal contest on the African coast, as witnessed in 1949. A wandering hippo came across a 136kg (300lb) blue pointer shark basking in the shallows. The dozy shark didn't know what had hit it when it was hurled up onto the beach and trampled on.

Blind Faith

A virtually blind bloodhound tracked down more than 100 criminals for US police in the 1930s. With an ultra-keen sense of smell more than making up for his poor eyesight, Old Boston could follow a criminal scent across any terrain.

Terrier Spirit

A fox terrier called Whiskey beat the odds with one of the most intrepid canine journeys ever recorded. Whiskey, aged 8 in 1973, became separated from her owner – Geoff Hancock – near Darwin in Australia's Northern Territory but was reunited with him months later after a gruelling journey of 2,720km (1,690 miles) through some of the most inhospitable country in Australia. Exhausted Whiskey even braved the great central wilderness.

Mountain Mutt

Some of the greatest Alpine mountains were conquered in the late 19th century, not by pioneering mountaineers but a dog. Before she died, Tschingel (named after the Swiss village in which she was born) made 53 major ascents. She accompanied the Rvd. William Coolidge on all the major peaks of her home Bernese Oberland region, such as the Eiger and the Jungfrau, which were around 4,000m (13,000ft) high. As an honorary member of the Alpine Club, the peak of her climbing exploits came in 1875, just prior to her death, in conquering the highest mountain in Europe, Mont Blanc – 4,808m (15,775ft). And she wasn't even a Pyrenean mountain dog!

13 Mixed Blessings

One of the more bizarre doggy liaisons came in 1972 through the mating of a Great Dane bitch and a dachshund male. Experts couldn't agree if the resulting puppies were "Great Dachshunds" or "Little Danes" but all of the 13-strong litter had short legs like Dad!

Cat Lottery Winner

If black cats are lucky, then that was certainly true of Blackie, who belonged to recluse Ben Rea, who was living in Britain. He shunned relatives to leave his £10m ($15m) fortune to his faithful cat. Blackie inherited the cash bonanza on Rea's death in 1988 as did various cat charities. That meant years in the lap of luxury, not only for Blackie but other moggies, too.

Three Out of Nine Gone!

A cat survived three shipwrecks in just six months during World War Two – and it didn't matter which side he was on! First, Oscar's sympathies were German when he rode the high seas on the mighty battleship Bismarck until it sank in 1941. The bedraggled moggy was pulled to safety by the crew of the Royal Navy destroyer *HMS Cossack*, but this association proved short-lived as *Cossack* was also sunk, six months later in the Atlantic Ocean. Oscar was rescued again and transferred to ratting duties on *HMS Ark Royal*, but just three days later, ended up in the water again when the aircraft carrier was torpedoed in the Mediterranean. He was found clinging for dear life to a wooden plank, where he had been stranded for three hours. The Navy decided that with just six lives left, Oscar needed to retire from active service and so the rest of his time was spent in the peace and quiet of a sailors' rest home in Northern Ireland.

Fur to Riches Story

A cat had to be relocated because of death threats over the fortune she inherited in 2003. Tinker was moved from England to Wales because widow Margaret Layne, whom Tinker had befriended, left £512,000 ($800,000), along with a trust fund of £145,000 ($226,000) to the moggy. Margaret didn't even own the cat who regularly visited her home.

A Taste for Religion

In 1949, termites destroyed priceless furniture and rare books at the heart of the Roman Catholic faith in the Vatican.

Lucy Kitty

A fortune left in a will to two cats called Brownie and Hellcat just kept on growing despite the beneficiaries being long dead. They were left $415,000 (£260,000) each by American doctor William Grier in the 1960s. However, because the money was invested wisely, by the 21st century the cats' legacy, largely unused, was worth a cool $4.1 million (£2.5 million).

Waving a Tail

The surfing exploits of a dog proved an Internet hit in 2011. Mango, a two-year-old labrador, was a popular YouTube choice after being taught to surf at Newquay in Cornwall, England by Matt Slater.

Bird Brain Idea

Seagulls and bread were bizarre British secret weapons during World War II. Submariners would release bread onto the surface attracting flocks of wheeling and screaming gulls. Gulls would then associate a long dark underwater shadow with food and when sharp-eyed observers saw a flock in a position where there was no known friendly sub, they knew it would be an enemy and swiftly implemented countermeasures.

Monkey Business

A drunken man who upset a troop of monkeys by swimming in their pool got more than he bargained for at a zoo in São Paulo, Brazil. Indignant about this boozy primate invading their territory, they sent him packing with a few bites in 2011.

Peg Goes Home

A dog that escaped the horrors of war in Afghanistan went home to Britain – but without his paratrooper master. Conrad Lewis adopted the dog while on a tour of duty in 2010 and the pair were inseparable, and Lewis planned for them to return to the UK together. Sadly he was killed in action and didn't make it home, but Peg (named after the Pegasus flying horse emblem of the British Parachute Regiment) found a new home in England. The soldier's family paid £4,000 ($6,300) to fly the beloved pet home, where she was given a resounding and tearful welcome.

Bugged Bunnies

A couple devoted to their rabbits wanted to keep an eye on them while holidaying in 2011 so they spent £1,000 ($1,580) on a sophisticated spy system. High-tech CCTV meant Jason and Mairi Batterbee from England could go online via a smartphone to see if Hunnie and Runnie were OK. Of course the rabbits were fine because their high-tech hutch was fitted with air conditioning and LED lighting, too!

Bentley's Collie Wobbles

A nervous dog had to have specially-made mittens when a nail-biting habit got out of hand. Bentley the cowardly border collie developed, and was unable to get over, a host of fears after his owner died. He took to chewing his feet out of fear of abandonment and was also afraid of the dark, doorbells and cats meowing.

Eye Of the Tiger

Vets were faced with one of their more unusual tasks when they saved the sight of a rare white tiger. Zena already lost one eye to the disease glaucoma in 2005 and faced complete blindness in 2011, when a cataract grew on the other. Surgeons carried out a successful operation to remove the cataract.

On Me Trunk, Son!

Maya the elephant became the star of a sanctuary in India for her nifty footballing skills and at 40 she is not over the hill. She developed a powerful shot with her trunk and when staff at the Wildlife SOS centre in Agra tried to stop her shots, they ended up in the net as well!

Escape Claws

A buzzard who swapped soaring among the thermals in the air for the underground life had to be rescued at Lydney, Gloucestershire in 2011. Rescue teams had to go more than 11m (36ft) down a disused mine shaft after the bird of prey became trapped below ground.

Anti-Smoking Crusader

Showbiz elephant Anna May hated people smoking. If a fellow film cast member so much as reached for a cigarette packet, she would confiscate them with her trunk and promptly eat them.

Living High On the Dog

German shepherd dog Gunther IV became the world's richest pet in 2009 when he inherited a hefty $370m (£240m). The fortune came from his father, Gunther III, who was the beloved pet of German countess and animal lover Karlotta Liebenstein. On her death, her money was left to Gunther III, whose line has continued to benefit from the bequest. Thanks to wise investments, the fortune left to Gunther IV had tripled by the 21st century. At the time of writing, he was enjoying the best of everything in food and accommodation. The latest Gunther had even purchased a villa in Miami, Florida from singer Madonna and won a very rare white truffle in a raffle. By comparison, a poodle called Toby Rimes was a comparative pauper with just $92m (£58m) in 2011. He was the direct descendant of a poodle that inherited $30m (£19m) from Ella Wendel, a New York socialite who died in 1931.

Purr-fect!

Smokey the cat achieved a world-record loud purr in 2011 with an impressive 67.7 dB. Owner Lucinda Adams of Pitsford, Northamptonshire, England got Smokey in a relaxed purr-fect mood for the record attempts with a grooming brush, slices of ham and stroking by hand. The measurement was taken from a distance of 1m (3.2ft).

On the Move

One of the biggest concentrations of dolphins ever spotted was in the 1950s, when observer aircraft estimated 100,000 were migrating in a single school in the Russian Black Sea.

True Horsepower

Horses are a regular sight in Louisville, but one driving a huge red American car certainly stopped the traffic in the state of Kentucky. Butterscotch the palomino was taught to drive a 1962 Lincoln Continental by his trainer, Ham Morris. It took 18 months for the 750kg (1,600lb) horse to master driving the car, which was specially adapted to allow him to operate the controls with his hoofs. Morris reported that Butterscotch was the second horse he has trained to drive.

What a Let Down!

A bloodhound employed in the 1930s by police in New England, USA slavishly followed a criminal all night and successfully drove the hunted man up a tree. The bloodhound stayed at the foot of the tree all night long, waiting for "back-up" from his human police colleagues, but they had gone home for the night. Frustrated and fed-up, the tenacious dog eventually did the same and the story only came out years later when the criminal, caught for another offence, recounted his uncomfortable night up the tree.

Rug Snacks

A kindly British army officer ordered pack mules to be rugged up on a very cold night. However, the animals belonging to the Army Mule School took them to be midnight snacks and ate the lot except for the buckles! The mules were unharmed except for one which did swallow a buckle and died.

Millionaire Monkey

The title of "world's richest ape" was snatched from under the nose of Kalu the Congolese chimpanzee. He was about to be worth an estimated £40m ($63m) as one of the heirs to the fortune of eccentric aristocrat Patricia O'Neill, but in 2011 Mrs O'Neill, 85, revealed that her fabulous wealth had been embezzled and she was penniless. O'Neil, the daughter of the Countess of Kenmore, lived with Kalu, 30 dogs and 11 cats on a sprawling estate near Cape Town, South Africa.

Faithful to the Last

A little dog stayed with Mary Queen of Scots to the very end of her life. It was found covered in blood in the folds of her long gown after the Queen was convicted of treason and beheaded at Fotheringay Castle, England in 1587. Even after being discovered, the Skye terrier refused to leave his mistress. The regal dress of the time contained many layers of cloth and so it was easy for the small pet to have hidden there. Finally, the dog – whose name has not been recorded in the annals of Tudor history – was taken away and washed by ladies-in-waiting.

Sticky Problem

In 2010, an X-ray showed a dog living in the USA had swallowed an entire tube of glue, but it wasn't easy to spot because the tube had formed itself into a perfect stomach shape. Vets performed an operation to remove it and the dog displayed no long-term ill effects.

Titanic Slice of Luck

Two passenger dogs survived the sinking of the *Titanic*, in which 1,517 died. The liner quickly sank after hitting an iceberg in the North Atlantic Ocean in 1912, but no one seemed to have objected to the dogs being taken into the lifeboats. Miss Margaret Hays of New York kept her little Pomeranian with her, while Henry Harper saved Sun Yat Sen, his Pekinese.

Wow! Take a Bow

A Hollywood star once received 10,000 letters per week – and didn't read one of them. The popularity of canine movie star Rin Tin Tin, who made 26 motion pictures for Warner Brothers between 1918 and 1932, far outweighed that of top human actors of the time.

Long & Active Life

The longest-surviving dog on record was an Australian Cattle Dog, who lived to be just over 29 years old. Bluey, who worked herding cattle and sheep on a farm in Victoria State, Australia, lived from 1910-39.

No Pressure, Then?

The pressure was well and truly on for a cat named Amber, who was appointed to Glenturret Distillery, near Crieff in Perthshire, Scotland in 1987. She followed world-record holding mouser Towser, whose count was 28,899 over 24 years. Unfortunately, Amber didn't seem to have her predecessor's skills and as far as is known, she never caught a single mouse although she remained as the resident feline until her death from old age in 2004.

Are Roo Human?

A kangaroo was truly living the high life as a human in 2011 – complete with suit, tie and his own bed to sleep in. Irwin, the partially paralysed great red kangaroo, was the favourite of Oklahoma animal shelter owner Christie Carr and he lived in her home. Weighing 11kg (24lb), he was dressed in human clothes and slept in Christie's bed, where he had a habit of hogging the pillows. Irwin, who ran into a fence when he was young and fractured his neck, was a local star and was a regular visitor at a neighbourhood nursing home.

Photogenic Innards

The contents of a stomach are not normally the favourite to win a photo competition – unless you happen to be a dog with nine billiard balls inside. In 2011, the unnamed dog won America's Wackiest X-rays contest in the *Veterinary Practice News* magazine. The dog was brought into Bayshore Animal Hospital in Oregon by his owners after they noticed him going lame while playing fetch. Swallowing the balls was soon found to be the real problem when a vet felt his abdomen for abnormalities. An operation to retrieve them proved successful and the dog subsequently regained his health.

Sinking Teeth In

Phillip Jay and Bridget Taylor loved touring the picturesque canals of Britain on their boat until they acquired a German shepherd dog. When left alone for a while, he bit through the glass-fibre hull and sank the boat!

Nipper's Hot Stuff!

A collie called Nipper refused to accept the word "hopeless" when a barn at a Sussex farm caught fire in 1985 with sheep and cattle trapped inside. Farm workers were unable to get close to the inferno to save them, but Nipper had other ideas. Time and again, he braved the flames and smoke to shepherd all the trapped animals out, even though he had singed fur and blistered paws.

Bird Accents

Just as a British accent from Birmingham sounds different to an English West Country burr, so too can birds according to a major study in 2011. Scientists found that city-dwelling birds developed different accents from their country cousins. Research by the University of Aberystwyth in Wales found birds of all species adapted their calls and song to get over echoes caused by buildings, particularly high-rise blocks.

Larry's a Victim of Politics

Loyalty in politics is always thin on the ground, even for a cat. In 2011, British Prime Minister David Cameron barred a cat called Larry from his new apartment at 10 Downing Street. It seemed Larry, brought in to catch the many mice around the historic centre of British politics, had been lying down on the job. Far from nabbing mice, he had spent much of his time sleeping or rubbing around the legs of visiting world leaders and dignitaries.

Croc Bites Mower

A crocodile launched an attack on a lawnmower that seemed to annoy him at a zoo in Australia. Elvis the croc suddenly snatched the mower from the grasp of terrified keepers at Somersby, near Sydney and dragged the machine into his pool.

Cocker Whoop

A crossbred cocker spaniel/poodle called Alfie won the title of Britain's Happiest Dog in 2011. The broad grin and furiously wagging tail of the nine-month-old "cockapoo" from Bristol won over the judges who made him top of the 75 other dogs in the competition.

Property Mognate

A cat called Tommaso inherited £6m ($10m) of property when his owner died in 2011. Apartments and houses the length and breadth of Italy went to the cat according to the will of a 94-year-old widow once married to a construction company owner.

Roam-eo & Juliet

Stray cats formed the cast of a bizarre version of *Romeo & Juliet* by Belgian director Armando Acosta in 1989. A white long-haired Turkish angora female played Juliet, while the grey cat cast as Romeo was only weeks before found close to death and had been nursed by Acosta.

Delayed By Dog

A frightened whippet brought costly chaos to Manchester Airport, England in 2011. The dog managed to elude security staff and got onto the runway, which meant the airport had to be closed to flights. One flight from Turkey was diverted 160km (100 miles) away to Birmingham, while 12 others were forced to circle as the dog, capable of speeds of up to 35mph, was rounded up and returned to its family, unhurt.

S-s-s-sexy Snake!

A sleeping woman at Krakow in Poland thought her boyfriend was being affectionate when she felt something wrap round her thigh. She got the shock of her life when she fully woke up to find 2m-long (6ft 6in) escaped snake wrapped around her upper leg!

Herd of This?

In 2011, cows featured as guests in the wedding photographs of a couple in Wales. Beef farmer Michael Hanson and his new wife Hayley posed with the herd at their cow-themed wedding of 2011.

Cropping Budgets

Exmoor ponies were the beneficiaries of crisis-enforced budget cuts in England. The South Tyneside Council, which needed to trim £35m ($55m) from its costs in 2011, drafted in the ponies as lawnmowers at the Cleadon Hills Nature Reserve and cut grass cutting costs by a third.

Short Trip

Missing cat Willow was found in 2011, just 32km (20 miles) from her home in Devon, England. Despite being relatively close to home, she had disappeared for four years.

Fat Chance!

Cassie the dog enjoyed a new lease of life in 2011 when she lost a massive 30kg (63lb) in a human-style diet. The collie had ballooned to 57kg (125lb) because her elderly owner in Warwickshire, England fed her inappropriate food, including full English fried breakfasts, takeouts, chocolate and roast dinner. After her owner, who genuinely loved Cassie, was taken into care, the now morbidly-obese bitch was transferred to an animal centre, where caring staff realized her life was at risk and reduced her intake to two bowls of healthy food a day plus a regime of walks and treadmill sessions. Her owner had not realised that many of the foods humans eat are actually harmful to pets.

Love Conquers All

A turkey escaped the Christmas dinner table in 2011 because it became infatuated with a deer at an animal rescue centre in Warwickshire, England. Tinsel the turkey fell off a lorry that was taking him to a slaughterhouse, then became inseparable from Bramble the deer.

How Op-skewer?

A Staffordshire bull terrier survived for four months after swallowing a 12cm (5in) kebab skewer in 2011. Vets saved the young dog's life with an emergency operation.

Nothing to Crow About

Postmen had nothing to fear from dogs when they delivered to the Weissmann home in Germany because the threat was aerial. After it fell from its nest, the family hand-reared a carrion crow chick and named it Jacob. As he grew, Jacob felt he had a duty to guard the home and regularly dive-bombed the postman, snatching letters from his grasp and then settling on a nearby roof to rip them open.

World Prayed For Star

One of the biggest worldwide media stories of early 2012 was Star the dog, found buried alive after being shot 40 times in the head. Tragic crossbreed Star won the hearts of millions of pet lovers after she was found whimpering in a shallow grave in Malta with just her nose protruding. After her muzzle was tightly bound, she had been shot and then buried in the ground with a board on top of her. The plucky Star survived despite having more than 40 pellets removed from her head.

Snow Much Fun!

When the first of the winter snow arrives, the fun starts for monkeys in the Jigokudani National Park. The aptly-named Japanese snow monkeys have learned to mimic humans and not only mould snow into balls, but also stage snowball fights.

Jealous Guys

Penguins showed their dismay at the arrival of pandas at Edinburgh Zoo in Scotland by pooing on visitors who flocked to see the bears. Tian Tian and Yang Guang were so popular on their arrival in late 2011 that queues of people built up, ignoring the rockhopper penguins nearby. In a black-and-white case of jealousy, the penguins seized attention by bombing visitors with foul-smelling droppings!

Elvis Impersonator

A new monkey type with a distinctive Elvis Presley hairstyle was discovered in 2011. The "King" look-alikes were among 208 previously unknown species found by scientists in a remote region of the Mekong Delta in southern Vietnam and Myanmar.

Where To, Deer?

Dobbey the reindeer enjoyed the freedom of the London suburb of Enfield in 2011. The hand-reared deer, eight, was taken into town by owner Gordon Elliott in a specially adapted London cab and strolled down the local high street on a lead. Dobbey travelled on the London Underground system, loved visiting the pub with his owner and even attended church on Christmas morning.

Supersize Litter

Even animals do things in a big way in the state of Texas. A female cat called Dusty was reputed to have had 420 kittens during her lifespan of 17 years.

Property Dog

German shepherd dog Viking Baron von Heppepiatz acquired a fortune as exaggerated as his name when he inherited property worth £130,000 ($200,000) from his property tycoon owner in 1971.

Loyal Follower

Forgiving tom Rusty had no intention of being abandoned by his neglectful owner in 1949. The brave ginger cat hit the road from Boston, Massachusetts and followed his owner a record 1,530km (950 miles) all the way to Chicago, Illinois – and he did so in an amazing 83 days!

Squawk Talk

Parrots proved unlikely allies for a politician in India during an election of 1996. The candidate trained a flock of them to squawk his name and then sent them out to rural parts of his constituency literally to get his name spread about.

No Cat-achism

On a Sunday in 1803, a cat was fired for working. A priest threw the cat out of church in England for catching a mouse during the service. Nine other cats that didn't follow suit were allowed to stay.

Concrete Kitty

A kitten cemented its place in animal folklore after surviving being buried in concrete. It slipped into wooden shuttering prepared for the concrete and was trapped for 53 hours in 1974. When the concrete had set, workers removed the shuttering and found the small creature had survived on air allowed in by cracks in the wood. They also discovered the concrete had set into an exact kitten body shape!

Security Stripes

It seemed a great step forward in security – get a tiger to guard money. It would take a very brave criminal to try a heist but having a tiger guard also had its drawbacks. During the 1980s, a New Zealand bank stored up to $50,000 (£32,000) at a time in the cage of a tiger at Auckland Safari Park. For two weeks, this seemed a great solution until customers complained of their notes smelling of tiger sweat and other big cat odour. A deodorant spray failed to completely eradicate the pong, so the experiment was abandoned.

Sub-aqua Cat

A marine cat went down with his ship but survived for eight days underwater. Peter was the resident rat catcher on a Dutch ship in 1964 when it capsized on the River Rhine in Germany. Luckily he found an air pocket and managed to hold his head above the water until he was rescued more than a week later.

Getting Sleigh-ed

An elephant that substituted for a reindeer in pulling a Santa Claus sleigh was not asked back. Lola the five-year-old pachyderm was spooked as she drew the sleigh around Eastbourne, England and left a trail of havoc in her wake. Careering around the streets, she eventually destroyed the sleigh. Having tipped the terrified Santa out, she burst free of her reins, damaged cars and eventually came to a halt after smashing her way through doors into the lobby of a hotel.

Jump To It!

If an animal Olympic Games were ever to be held, a German shepherd dog called Crumstone Danko would be a two-event legend. Back in the 1940s, he achieved a high-jump record of 3.43m (11ft 3in) over a wall and was a sensational long jumper as well, once leaping 7.3m (24ft).

Littered With Cats

Cat lovers Donna and Jack Wright once lived with 689 moggies in their home in Ontario, Canada. They kept on taking in strays until they reached this massive total, who munched their way daily through 180 giant cans of pet food and 25kg (55lb) of dried cat food, washed down by 5.9l (10.5pt) of milk. Every morning at 5.30, Donna began cleaning out ten giant cat litter trays.

Living In Style

A family of spinster sisters dedicated all their affections to poodle dogs. The super-wealthy Wendle sorority had a number of them at their New York mansion at the turn of the 20th century and each enjoyed a diet of tender lamb chops and slept in his own specially-made hand-carved bed. Fearing fortune hunters, the reclusive sisters shunned men and marriage and to them, their dogs were everything.

Haring About the Streets

Shoppers in an English town centre in 2011 were amazed to see not only a rabbit hopping around – but a giant rabbit. The bunny, at 60cm (2ft) and 8kg (18lb) was larger than many breeds of dog. Nicknamed "Thumper", the rabbit was taken into care by a vet in Swindon, Wiltshire, who declared it fit and healthy, and rehoused it in a dog kennel. It was thought Thumper had become a victim of recession-biting Britain at the time and was abandoned by owners who could no longer afford to feed it.

Fat Cats

In 1980, the British government led by Prime Minister Margaret Thatcher revealed it had more than 100,000 cats on the Civil Service payroll, most of them on pest control duties.

Bee-ing the Best

The world record, as at 2011, for attracting bees on to a naked human body was 83.5kg (184lb). People's Republic of China citizen Zhang Wei was the champion bee-wearer.

Living High On the Hog

A pig that became a favourite at a sanctuary for injured animals lived in a brick-built house – called "Pigmalion" – at Gwent in South Wales and enjoyed strawberry milkshakes every day. Ben, adopted by Maria Hennessy, also had a worldwide fan club.

Walkies!

Police soon put a stop to a lazy dog-sitter's attempt to avoid exercising her charge without any effort. The woman from Boulder, Colorado drove her Toyota car while a tiny Chihuahua ran alongside at 15mph. Although the dog struggled to keep up, it was unhurt by the experience but the dog-sitter was quite rightly charged with animal cruelty in 2011.

Travelling Fur Life

Princess Truman Tao-Tai became the most travelled cat in the world in 1975 after 1.5m sea miles. The Siamese joined a British iron-ore carrier ship as a kitten and trainee rat catcher in 1959 and stayed on board, visiting dozens of different countries until 1975, with 2.4 million kilometres (1.5m miles) under her collar.

Dogs Do a Good Turn

Super-fit dogs were a vital part of any English kitchen for a few years after the Tudor times of the 16th century when they were used in the predecessor to hamster wheels to turn roasting spits. Requiring energy and stamina, there was even a special dog breed for the job, appropriately titled "the turnspit". Believed to be a relative of the Glen of Imaal terrier, the turnspit breed was eventually extinct by the 19th century.

Champion Catcher

One of the greatest ratters ever recorded in Britain was a cat that lived at the White City stadium in London between 1927 and 1933. She kept the venue free of 12,480 rats but could not fully take her place in the annals of animal history because the female tabby's name appears not to have been recorded.

Putting His Feet Up

A horse that liked to sleep on his back with four feet in the air caused much consternation from folk passing his field in Surrey, England in the 1990s. Fearing Roger the gelding was dead, concerned passers-by kept contacting his owner, farmer Philip Davis. After a considerable number of calls, Phil put up a notice saying "Don't worry. This horse is NOT dead."

Lucky Leg Break

A surgeon who kept his cool eventually inherited a multi-million dollar fortune – just for repairing a dog's broken leg. Although known for his brilliance for treating humans at a New York hospital, Dr Brian Gibney answered a call from the mansion of the super-wealthy Wendle family in the early 20th century to find the victim of a broken leg was a poodle named Toby. He set aside his annoyance at being misled and treated Toby over several months until the dog was completely healed. When the last of the Wendle family of property tycoons died, some decades later, Gibney found himself richer by several million dollars.

Steer Crazy

A feisty steer on his way to a rodeo couldn't wait to get started and busted out of his trailer to cause havoc. He halted traffic on a major road near Yuma, Arizona, and then leapt over a brick wall. Following this, he turned his attention to police vehicles and, according to a police spokesman, "kicked the crap out of them" before being successfully lassoed.

Odin's Odd For a Tiger

Zoo staff found a rare tiger also had a rare talent – he loved water. Odin the 3m-long (10ft) white Bengal tiger loved diving into a pool and swimming powerful strokes at a zoo near San Francisco, California. Cats of all sizes generally hate getting wet, but Odin's remarkable skill was discovered when some meat fell into the pool and he dived in after it. He actually had the ability to close his nostrils.

Surfing Dogs

Taking like ducks to the water every year since 2008 have been a host of water-loving dogs. They and their owners flock to Huntingdon Beach, California for the annual Surf City Surf Dog competition. Dogs of all sizes, breeds and weights take to the Pacific Ocean surf and some compete for world records, such as Most Dogs on a Board and Longest Ride by a Dog.

Animal Vacation

For many centuries in the county of Somerset in England, the Twelfth Night of Christmas has traditionally been a day off for working animals such as horses and cattle. Many farmers and homesteads present their animals with special treats in their food as a present.

Spoilsport Gulls

A football pitch was rendered unplayable in 2010 by a flock of seagulls on a feeding frenzy. The water table on the pitch on the Channel island of Guernsey was high and worms were near the surface so the gulls paddled their feet up and down to tease the creatures out. St Martin's AC was forced to cancel games or play them elsewhere while it spent hundreds of pounds re-turfing the pitch after this aerial vandalism.

Rat Attack

In a record unlikely ever to be beaten in the 21st century, a bull terrier killed 500 rats in 93 minutes. Jenny Lind claimed the title of Greatest Ratter in the World in 1833, in a Liverpool pub competition (these events are no longer held).

Claw Strolls

The French poet, essayist and translator Gérard de Nerval amazed 19th-century Paris by strolling through the city with a pet lobster. "Thibault" became a familiar sight being led by the eccentric Romantic movement poet on the end of a blue silk ribbon through the gardens of the Palais Royal in the French capital.

No Luck for King

A black cat was subject to 24-hour armed security because its royal owner believed this would bring him luck. Charles I of England arranged for the cat to be guarded day and night, but in a strange twist of fate, it died on the day before Oliver Cromwell's troops arrested the king. With the cat, the tyrant king's luck died, too, as Charles was beheaded in 1649 after a civil war.

Softly-softly Software

A company came up with a solution to cats crashing computers by walking on keyboards. Arizona firm BitBoost's PawSense software can differentiate between cat paws and human fingertips on a computer keyboard. The secret lies in the fact that cat's paws depress two or three adjacent keys at once – the application also plays an irritating sound to shoo pussy off!

Cats Dictate to Dictators

Some of the most violent men in history had one thing in common – a fear of cats. Dictators Adolf Hitler, Napoleon Bonaparte and Alexander the Great all hated cats.

Feline Lifesavers

The superior instincts of cats helped the people of London throughout World War Two. Cats were lifesavers during the Blitz on Britain in the early 1940s because their acute hearing enabled them to sense enemy aircraft before humans were able to. The sight of cats running to hide was a cue for their owners to head for the air-raid shelters.

High Life

A cat ran up a tree and stayed there for six years. Mincha took to the high life when she ran up a 12m (40ft) tree in the Argentinian capital of Buenos Aires during the 1940s and decided not to come down. That's hardly surprising since the kind-hearted locals pushed food up to her on a pole and a milkman delivered daily. The eccentric Mincha also managed to give birth to several kittens up there but it is not known whether she came down to meet her suitors or if they made the climb to her high-rise home.

Doggy Dividends

American oil heiress Eleanor Ritchley left $4.3m (£2.7m) to her 161 dogs in 1968 – that was about $26,000 per animal!

Moke Joke

In 2011, a donkey was ready to make an ass of the election process in Bulgaria. Campaigners pledged to put the creature up for the mayoral elections in Varna because, according to a spokesman, "Marko the donkey doesn't lie or steal like his rivals!"

Crazy Croc Work

Cost-cutting health officials in the 1980s decided to put man-eating crocodiles to work clearing up sewers in Manzini, Swaziland. The idea was that the crocs would be introduced into sewers to gobble up refuse. It had the secondary benefit of reducing the number of man-eaters in the local rivers – making the waters safer to cross!

Waiting For a Bite

It is no sweat for large snakes such as pythons if they can't lay their fangs on a meal as often as they would like. They have been known to go 570 days, 18 months without food before eating and then going without food for another 415 days. According to scientists one snake was observed to survive 679 days, over two years, on liquids alone.

Cat Alarm

The sharp end of a cat's claws saved an American trawler captain from certain fiery death. Gus Dunsky was asleep and unaware the *Whitecap* was ablaze until the ship's cat Lizzie jumped through flames and smoke to alert him to the danger.

Taxman Tries to Bite Dog

A sheepdog called William ended up in a long drawn-out court battle with Britain's Inland Revenue over his earnings. William's problem was that a share trading account run by his investment analysis owner Robert Beckman had amassed a fortune of more than £100,000 ($158,000). The British taxman tried to relieve William of £30,000 ($47,000) in Capital Gains Tax, but a court ruled against this and the claim was duly dropped.

Truly a Sheep-dog!

A lamb called Jack might have been described as baa-rking mad because he was not sure if he was dog or sheep. In 2011, Jack was brought up by a Springer spaniel after being abandoned by his mother and this led to a split personality. Owner Alison Sinstadt of Market Drayton in England said Jack fetched sticks, stood on his hind legs and tried to bark with a half-baa, half-woof. Faced with a flock of sheep, like any good spaniel he even tried to round them up!

Elephant Problem Solver

An elephant's brain proved better than man's when one of the creatures amazed observers with its problem-solving and life-saving ability. Elephants working in Burma in the 1940s had to balance huge logs across their tusks and hoist them 3m (10ft) onto a raised platform. One elephant could see what its handlers couldn't – that a log could roll off the platform, killing its driver who was perched behind the elephant's ears. Of its own volition, the tusker searched out a smaller and longer stake and wedged it vertically so that it would check any rolling logs.

Measuring Up

A waiting game was required after attempts to measure a giant crocodile failed in North Borneo. The croc was believed to be 200 years old and locals were so frightened of it that they threw money into the Seguma River to ward off its "evil influence". They believed he was a record size but couldn't get near enough to prove it. One day in the 1950s, he was by chance seen basking on a sandbank, which just about accommodated his vast size. When he moved away, the bank was measured at 9.9m (32ft) long.

Inside Job

Cops in Brixton, south London were mystified by a series of thefts from bags inside their own police station. However, detectives put on the job to make internal inquiries soon found the culprit: a guard dog named Duke, who was wolfing down whatever he could find.

Kicking Off

Mr Bean the mule literally kicked off when ambushed by Japanese soldiers in Burma during World War II. While returning from carrying a load of signalling wire to the front line in 1944, Mr Bean was abandoned by his party of soldiers when they ran into the Japanese patrol. This seemed to pique his temper and he ran at the Japanese, liberally kicking out at them. Later, when Mr Bean returned to camp, it was found that he had taken a bullet in the ribs but showed no signs of discomfort.

Acting the Goat

A prolific goat thief had a unique way of getting away with his crimes. He would steal goats from rural areas of Ghana in Africa, dress them up in human clothes and drive them away in a Ford Escort, all the while pretending to be a family out for a ride. His downfall came in the 1990s when police thought the family inside dressed in T-shirts was very ugly and decided on a spot-check.

Tortoise Prisoner

A tortoise that became a turncoat after being taken as a prisoner of war lived for more than 100 years. He was happily living the life of a Frenchman as a mascot for a garrison on the island of Mauritius, but was taken "prisoner" when the British ousted Napoleon's troops in 1810. The creature was well looked after and despite going blind in 1908, lived on for another 10 years. Even then, he only died by accident when he fell down a gun emplacement, aged a definite 152. Another estimate was that he was around 180 because the French explorer Chevalier de Fresne had recorded taking the tortoise from his native Seychelles to Mauritius in 1766.

Squawky Clean

Two parrots became so attached to their owner Stuart Romain that they even showered with him. In 2011, cockatoo Coco and eclectus parrot Taz were his constant companions at his home in Yeovil, England and liked nothing better than a warm shower with him.

Trail Blazer

A joke backfired expensively on a man who thought he had killed a kangaroo in a road crash in Australia. Believing the creature to be dead, Emilio Tarra dressed it up in a Gucci blazer with the intention of taking a souvenir photo. But the hardy roo was just stunned and woke up to make a run for it, back to the Outback. Unfortunately, the blazer contained Emilio's passport, A$2,000 (£1,000) in cash and 16 credit cards!

Snappy Earner

The mean instincts of the alligator-snapping turtle were put to macabre use during the 20th century in Indiana, USA when their carrion-craving instincts were used to find the bodies of people who had drowned in lakes. The turtle was tied to a boat, and if it sensed a corpse under the water then it would dive down to try to eat it, so pointing out the spot to human searchers.

Elephant Enemy

A man who tried to stop a herd of binge-drinking elephants from breaking into an Indian Army rum store didn't realize what heavyweight enemies he had made. They never forgot him and launched a dedicated hate campaign against the soldier. The boozy tuskers made repeated raids by smashing their way into camp and before going for the rum, they always made straight for the soldier's hut and demolished it.

Croc Freedom Battle

In 2011, animal rights activists fought a furious campaign to free the biggest-ever captured crocodile – even though the reptile was an alleged double killer. Lolong, who weighed a tonne and was 6.4m (21ft) long, was captured after two people disappeared in Bunawan, Philippines and was put on display as a tourist attraction. It took 30 men to take Lolong (believed to be the biggest saltwater croc ever captured), but animal rights campaigners representing People for the Ethical Treatment of Animals claimed it was cruel to keep him and demanded his release, even though he would still pose a threat to humans.

Farewell Bow... Wow!

A dog retired with a record for the most stage performances for a canine. Danny the Wheaten terrier became the world record holder when he took his final curtain in 2011. He had been playing Sandy in the British touring company of the musical *Annie* for 12 years and 1,365 performances when he retired. During his life as a thespian, he had a special dressing room and was rewarded with treats of cheese and sausages.

Cow Jumps Iron Curtain

Armed border guards and barbed wire proved no match for a determined cow in the 1970s. She defected from communist East Germany to the West by swimming 120 metres (130 yards) across the River Elbe – her exploit was officially recognized by the West German authorities when granted asylum.

Historical Croc

In 2011, palaeontologists found the skeleton of an extinct giant crocodile. Previously, excavations in the same Colombian mine had revealed the remains of the largest-ever snake at 13m (43ft). The croc, which competed with the titanoboa snake for food, was only half the size at 6.5m (21ft) but threw fresh light on the ecosystem of the New World Tropics in the Paleocene period.

Making a Meal of It

A Swiss peasant reacted quickly when in 1934 he found a ferocious big cat in a barn and promptly killed it with a wood axe. Unaware of what the creature was, he had cooked and eaten it before discovering it was actually a black panther which had escaped from a zoo!

Triggering Success

One of the most famous screen horses had more tricks up his sleeve than was ever seen in his films between the 1930s and the 1960s. Trigger, the golden palomino who partnered cowboy star Roy Rogers, could sign his name with an "X" holding a pen in his teeth. Among 60 other tricks were counting and doing simple addition and subtraction by stamping with his hooves and removing a six-gun from a holster with his teeth.

Law-Abiding Avians

Researchers found in 2012 that birds stick to a speed limit when flying. However, they are not afraid of speeding tickets, but of death. The Massachusetts Institute of Technology found birds must fly below a certain speed to avoid crashing into trees and other obstacles. With the absence of any helpful road signs, birds have to work out their safe maximum speed by taking into account factors such as their size and manoeuvrability, as well as how built-up the area is.

Cat Courted Danger

The Berlin Wall was just another wall for a cat named Putzi in the 1980s and so he hopped over it and found himself embroiled in an East-West diplomatic situation. He had climbed into the eastern zone and intransigent communist border guards threatened to shoot anyone trying to retrieve the cat in no-man's land. But his owner still risked his life for Putzi: while his children distracted the guards, he drilled a hole in the wall for his beloved pet to climb through to safety.

Ice-Cool Killer

Polar bears sometimes use tools to make a kill. They have been observed sneaking up behind sleeping walruses to kill them with a heavy chunk of ice. Scientists believe it is the polar bear's way of avoiding an open confrontation, which could lead to injuries.

Cheating Cheetahs

Cheetahs lived up to their name when racing them was first introduced in England in 1937. Although they can reach speeds of 110kph (68mph), the race organizers at Romford Greyhound Stadium in England reckoned without the crafty cats' lazy natures. One quickly worked out that it could simply lie and wait for the mechanical hare to come around to it. It was also found that once one cheetah took the lead, the others gave up. The cheetah racing idea, which was intended to boost flagging attendance figures, was never tried again.

Cat Mystery

Mystery surrounded a cat that was found 2,620km (1,628 miles) from its original home. Willow had been missing from his family in Colorado, in the American West, for five years but in 2011 was found on the East Coast in New York. The mystery was how the cat travelled 2,620km but showed no sign of a long overland trek on foot. Willow was clean, in good condition and even a little overweight. However he got to the Big Apple, he was reunited with his Colorado family by air.

Chicken Legs It!

A chicken was able to walk again after being fitted with a metal rod in her broken leg. Vets at Plumley in Cheshire, England carried out the operation.

Hogging the Space

A single six-acre garden once boasted more hedgehogs per hectare than any other part of Britain. The fact scores of them congregated there must surely be because the garden was at the home of Major Adrian Coles, who founded the British Hedgehog Preservation Society.

Cold Logic

A severe cold snap provided an escape opportunity for a polar bear in Chicago Zoo. The 270kg (600lb) female climbed the frozen arch of a water wall to make her escape from Lincoln Park Zoo. Her taste of freedom was short, however, as a keeper with a tranquilizer gun had already been alerted.

Love-a-Duck Hotel

Ducks take pride of place in one of the most prestigious hotels in the USA. Successive groups of five ducks, currently called Daisy, Daphne, Denise, Daffy and Donald, have occupied the fountain in the lobby of the Peabody Hotel in Memphis, Tennessee for 75 years. Now a tourist attraction, they waddle off for a twice-daily duck parade. The tradition started in 1932 when a group of hunters placed duck decoys in the fountain for a joke and the then-manager of the Peabody thought it a great idea to have real ducks.

Hell of a Shell

A tortoise thought to be 150 years old was discovered in 2011 on the Galapagos Islands in the eastern Pacific Ocean. It weighed 393kg (866lb).

Shy Type

A tiny creature that had been hiding for millions of years was discovered on the island of Madagascar. Scientists first identified the unknown species of mouse lemur in 2011 and christened it the "Gerp". It has a head the size of a human thumb.

Don't Feed the Bears!

The crew of a Canadian coastguard cutter made the mistake of being nice to a polar bear male – they just couldn't get rid of him. After floating up to the ship on an ice floe in 1969, the seamen threw black molasses and jam to the bear. But he came back for more and was not satisfied with a further "snack" of salt pork, peanut butter and salami. He spat out potatoes, apples and bread, but then decided to climb aboard after sampling chocolate. The 363kg (800lb) bear was now a danger to life but turning the ship's hoses on him merely provided an enjoyable warm shower for a beast used to sub-zero temperatures. Only the firing of noisy distress rockets sent him back to his ice floe.

Off to the Pub

A pet bearded dragon lizard, who went missing from his Leicestershire, England home in 2011, was found a month later at the George and Dragon pub at Seaton.

Now You See Me...

A species of seal disappeared for 50 years before revealing itself again. The Juan Fernandes of the Pacific Ocean were classified extinct by 1917, then rediscovered in 1968. Now the colony, which numbers hundreds, lives as a protected species on the islands they are named after on the west coast of Chile.

Under Par Puppy

A doberman dog ended up under par because of his love of golf balls. Zac, from Warwickshire, England, was close to death after swallowing five balls during walks on a golf course near his home. After 18 months with the balls lodged in his gut, he collapsed and needed immediate surgery. Luckily, it was successful.

Hat's the Way to Do It!

Playing cat and mouse proved a winner for British charities in the 1990s and at the turn of the 21st century. Fundraiser Snowy Farr was a regular feature in Cambridge's Market Square for a number of years as a cat sat on his top hat while several mice ran, unharmed, around the brim. Mr Farr raised £30,000 ($47,000) for charities and enough money for 17 guide dogs for blind people.

He Nose a Hunting Trick

When sneaking up on prey, polar bears hold their paws over the black nose to hide the only thing that isn't white in the Arctic landscape, which could give away their position.

Bombing Bats

A plan to recruit bats into the US Army during World War II ran into trouble because the boffins reckoned without the flying reptiles' continuous appetite for insects. The bats were to be trained to carry small firebombs behind enemy lines but the idea fell apart when the Army couldn't get enough insects for food.

Causing a Stink in Politics

Smelly the goat ran for mayor in the Brazilian town of Jaboata in 1955. Voters, sick of the corruption and laziness in local politics, voted the goat in with a 468 majority.

Rhino Relative

A skeleton found in 2011 revealed for the first time a rhinoceros with two horns had lived in the Himalaya region of Tibet 3.7 million years ago. The rhino was woolly 3.2m (10′5″) long and a vegetarian.

Pig-Headed Fan

A pig was red-carded when its owner tried to smuggle it into a Russian football match. Farmer and football fan Vladimir Kisilev from St Petersburg took his prize pig to a show in Moscow but at the same time wanted to see Zenit St Petersburg play a Moscow side in the Russian Premier League in 2009. Having nowhere to leave his prize pig, Vladimir tried to take it into the ground in a big bag but was undone by an inopportune grunt and both were thrown out of the ground.

Hero Baboon Went to War

A baboon did everything a brave soldier did to become a Great War hero. Chacma baboon Jackie, taken from his South Africa homeland for war service in France by his owner, Private Albert Marr, became a regimental mascot amid the horrors of the Western Front between 1916 and 1918. An excellent guard, Jackie stayed by Marr's side when he was wounded and even licked Marr's wounds until medics arrived. Later, Jackie was also wounded and lost a leg but recovered sufficiently to be promoted to corporal and the only monkey to get a medal for bravery. He returned to South Africa in 1918 and lived another three years.

Doggy Doc

A father and son were alive in 2011 because a specially trained cocker spaniel never left their side. Neil, 42, and eight-year-old son Jack had an aggressive type of diabetes, which left them prone to slipping into a coma at any time. With his ultra-sensitive sense of smell, Roots the spaniel had special revolutionary training to alert them if their blood sugar levels fluctuated and they risked falling into a hypoglycaemic coma; he had the ability to sniff out microscopic changes in the father and son's bodies.

Born Survivor

Thieves left a Staffordshire bull terrier for dead with 21 stab wounds but didn't allow for the animal's amazing strength of character. Dempsey's owner was away from her flat in Bournemouth, England when the robbery took place in 2011. Dempsey, described as gentle, was attacked with knives and left bloodied as the intruders escaped with their stolen goods. The vet who saved Dempsey described it as the worst case of dog injury he had ever seen but Dempsey made a full recovery.

Horn of a Dilemma

A protest vote led to a rhinoceros having a landslide council election win. Cacereo the female rhino polled 50,000 votes in São Paulo in 1959 but had to be thick-skinned about not being able to take her seat on the council. Officials managed to get the result declared void, but disillusioned voters took comfort in the fact that their political protests made headlines worldwide.

Locomotive Monkey

A monkey signalman was not an unusual sight for locomotive drivers in South Africa in the 1870s. Jack the chacma baboon helped a disabled station master and was taught how to sweep the station, change signals and look after the key for drivers to change points further up the line – and he was never paid a rand for all those years of dedicated work.

Hair Of the Dog

Dogs were not left out when their owners visited the pub at Newcastle-upon-Tyne, England in 2011. Publican Dave Carr of the Brandling Villa in South Gosforth attracted crowds of dog regulars with beefy non-alcoholic beer and a roast dinner with cat-flavoured gravy.

Water Feat

No dog was ever more aptly named than Neptune the Newfoundland after an incredible watery feat. The dog was on a boat being towed on the Mississippi River to New Orleans when he was pitched overboard. Unable to stop, Neptune's owner could only watch as his beloved pet faded into the watery distance. Imagine his shock and joy when Neptune paddled up to his moored craft to be reunited with him. He had paddled more than 80km (50 miles) in three days against strong tides and bad weather on the unpredictable American river.

Small and Very Loud

Pygmy marmosets might be the world's smallest monkeys but they are also big on noise. Loud whistles and squeals belie their 12cm (5in) length and 170g (6oz) weight and can be heard far and wide throughout their western Amazon rainforest habitat of South America.

Adder-ed to the Snake List

A seven-year-old British girl went down in wildlife history after the newest snake discovery in Africa was named after her. Matilda Davenport lent her name to the Matilda's horned viper, which was identified as a new species in 2011 by her wildlife expert father, Tim. The debutante viper is non-aggressive, about 60cm (2ft) long and although venomous, is not deadly.

Siamese Stroll

A cat that went missing seemed in no hurry to be reunited with its owners. Lost on holiday in South Wales in 1967, Ching the Siamese didn't catch up with his family in Gloucestershire, England until 1970 and had travelled at an estimated amble of only 160m (175 yards) a day.

Mini Mammal

The Kitti's hog-nosed bat is the smallest mammal known to man, being about the size of a US dime coin. Occupying only a small border area of Thailand and Myanmar, adults weigh 2g (0.07oz) and measure a miniscule 30–40mm (0.13in). Otherwise known as the bumblebee bat, they have large ears and noses resembling that of a pig.

Surprise Visitor

A tiny kitten embarked on an epic journey across England – and all for no reason. John Sutcliffe found the ginger traveller on his doorstep in 1973 and recognized it as the kitten he had bought for his granddaughter, three weeks earlier. It had barely settled in with its new family before it set off, covering 240km (150 miles) in 21 danger-filled days.

Was He, Wasn't He?

The British media became exercised in 2011 over the fate – or otherwise – of a majestic giant stag called the Emperor of Exmoor. For many years, it had lived unharmed in the Exmoor area of Devon until someone claimed they had shot the beast, who was a great favourite with many locals. A trophy head was then displayed at a local hotel, whose owner coyly claimed it "might" be the Emperor. Column centimetres and many media minutes continued to add up as the "is it, isn't it?" controversy raged. The man purported to have most photographed the Emperor insisted the trophy was the beast, while a local safari organizer who claimed to have seen the Emperor more frequently said it certainly wasn't. Meanwhile the trophy head was taken down from its place in the hotel. Only time and a live appearance of the big deer would end the saga and, at the time of going to print, the Emperor had not been seen.

Titans In a Flap

The great mythological titans met their match in 2011 – defeated by bats. Filming of the blockbuster movie *Clash of the Titans 2* had to go especially carefully because of the presence of a large colony of the rare lesser horseshoe bat. They happened to inhabit the part of the Brecon Beacons National Park in Wales that was preferred by the film producers because of its unique barren landscape. If there was any danger of the bats being disturbed, Liam Neeson and the rest of the crew had to stop filming.

Rule of Thumb

The Brookesia Minima chameleon is just the size of a human thumbnail. Among the smallest reptiles in the world, it measures just under 2cm (1in) in length. It hides amid the bark and leaves of the Madagascar jungle but looks the same as a full-sized chameleon, although a fraction of the size.

Fly Guy

The most beloved pet of the Roman poet Virgil was given a funeral that would have cost at today's prices around £50,000 ($75,000). Its ceremony included hire of human mourners to pay last respects, a full orchestra, long and moving speeches and love poems, plus a specially built mausoleum. All a bit excessive, perhaps as the favoured "pet" happened to be a housefly!

Don't I Know You?

Kind-hearted animal lover Barbara Paule took in a bedraggled cat that turned up at her home in Pennsylvania, USA in 1988, but soon began to think there was something familiar about it. It took her three days to realize that the cat had belonged to her years before. Muddy Water White had jumped out of Paule's stationary truck in 1985 when she was in Dayton, Ohio. It had taken the cat with an amazing sense of direction more than 1,000 days to travel 750km (450 miles).

Room to Graze

Stephen Noble had nowhere to graze his beloved pony, Grey Lady Too, so in 2011, he moved her into the front room of his home on the Scottish island of Lewis.

Tortoise On Parade

Police who rescued a tortoise from the fast lane of the M6 motorway in northern England were faced with an ownership dilemma. After the tale of Speedy's lucky escape hit the media, a rash of people claimed the tortoise as their own. The cops solved the mystery with an identity parade, in which they drafted in tortoises from a local nature park. Speedy's real owner Paul Dunn, 13, immediately picked out his pet.

Hitching a Ride

Separate studies have shown that London's pigeon population often save wing power by hitching lifts on the English capital's Underground train system. With the help of the human travelling public's observations, pigeons hopped into carriages and got off at will. In 1985, favourite destinations were Fulham Broadway and Parson's Green, but the birds also seemed to know when food was prolific at low tide on the River Thames by hopping off at Putney Bridge. In 1995, a further study found popular pigeon destinations were Baker Street and the appropriately avian-named Goldhawk Road.

Quailing at Migration

The mountain quail migrates such a short distance it is not even worth opening its wings. It walks from its summer nesting spot – 3,600m (12,000ft) up in the central Californian mountains – to its wintering altitude of 1,500m (5,000ft). When spring comes, the quails waddle in single file back up the mountain.

Dolphin 999 Squad

A school of dolphins were on the alert when a shark moved in to kill surfer Adam Maguire. The shark's first attack, off the Australian coast near Sydney, had already severely injured Adam before the dolphin 999 squad arrived. First they thrashed about to distract the shark and then they formed a protective shield around Adam, giving his friends enough time to pull him ashore. Adam recovered from the ordeal following emergency surgery and a blood transfusion.

High-Flying Moggie

A cat stowed away on a British Airways jumbo jet and covered 1 million km (600,000 miles) before being found. Hamlet was originally on a flight from Canada to England when his cage sprung open and he wandered off into the vast hold of the aircraft. A search failed to find him, but two months and hundreds of thousands of air miles later, Hamlet – owned by a family in Norfolk, England – was found safe behind panelling after trips to destinations that included Jamaica, Singapore, Australia and the Middle East.

Doggie Disputes

Pet dogs were in the dock in a 2011 lifestyle survey, when they were blamed for causing family rows across the UK. The survey by esure insurance company found dogs caused an average of 156 family rows over a year. Over an average dog lifespan of 13 years that added up to 2,028 disputes in total, it said.

Hare We Go

An errant hare achieved what many world-class defenders failed to do – outpace Bulgarian football superstar Hristo Stoichkov. The hare dashed onto the field of play at Barcelona FC's Camp Nou ground in 1990 and, in front of almost 100,000 people, caused Stoichkov to stumble and miss a goal opportunity. Much to the delight of the crowd, Stoichkov "hared" after the creature but failed to capture it.

One Good Tern...

An Arctic tern completed one of the greatest bird migration feats ever recorded when it travelled 22,400km (14,000 miles). The energetic bird was tagged in Russia in 1955 and later turned up in Western Australia.

Amazing Moggy

One of the gutsiest animal tales ever told was of a cat called Sugar who was born with a hip deformity. Although adopted by a neighbour when owner Stacy Wood moved from California to Oklahoma in 1952, Sugar couldn't bear to be parted and despite the painful hip, the cream Persian set out in search of Stacy after only two weeks. Even though Sugar had no idea whereabouts in Oklahoma her owner had moved to, she uncannily found her, some 14 months and 2,000km (1,250 miles) later after a painful pilgrimage during which she must have crossed the Rocky Mountains and the great American Desert.

Is It a Bird or an Insect?

The diminutive bee hummingbird is so small that it is often mistaken for an insect. However, it is the smallest bird in the world, weighing a mere 1.8g (0.063oz) and is 5cm (2in) long. The human retina cannot detect the rapid 80-beats-per-second movement of this Cuba native's extremely small wings. Its nest is smaller than a doll's teacup and its eggs smaller than coffee beans.

Pointer Dog

In 2011, a dog's flashing collar saved a man trapped on a flooded riverbank in England. Rescuers were able to spot the dog walker's pet's collar in the darkness at Dursley, Gloucestershire.

Sick as a Sent-Off Parrot

A red-faced parrot was red-carded at a football match. Me-Tu was attending an English amateur league match between Hatfield and Hertford Heath in 1995 with his owner when he began to imitate the referee's whistle. When the ref whistled, Me-Tu thought "me, too" but then got so good at it that he was confusing officials and players alike. Ref Gary Bailey soon found the culprit and owner Irene Kerrigan in the crowd and produced a red card.

Foxy Foot Fetish

Sports centre bosses were foxed by disappearing running shoes. More than 140 pairs went missing from outside the California gym, where they had been left to air after runs. But they were a delicious treat for a fox who loved the sweaty odour and carried them off to his lair as treasures. The mystery was solved when someone spotted the vulpine thief and followed him to his hideaway.

Reducing Toad Road Toll

Families in the picturesque English town of Petworth regularly came to the rescue of a colony of toads, which was in extreme danger. The toads needed to cross the busy A283 London Road to their breeding pond but there was often carnage as they adopted the strategy of trying to dodge the speeding wheels of many hundreds of vehicles per hour. In the 1990s, a group of concerned locals – at no small risk to themselves – ferried by hand in excess of 1,200 toads across the road. Later, pressure on the local council led to a safe toad tunnel being installed under the major road between Sussex and London. Naturally, toad survival rates went sky-high afterwards.

Fish in Space

The highest flying fish in history was a humble South American guppy, which went into space in 1976. As part of ongoing experiments the fish spent 48 days with the Russian crew of the Salyut 5 space station.

Lost In a Big Way

Despite having a formidable sense of direction, homing pigeons occasionally foul up. A bird released in the 1960s in France somehow lost track of its mission to fly to England and was found two months – and 12,000km (7,500 miles) – later in South Africa. It was one of the longest-ever flights recorded for a bird of that size.

Sea Ponies?

Seahorses that for decades were thought to be the young of a larger species kept a secret: they had an identity in their own right. The *Hippocampus denise*, barely discernible from the coral they inhabit off the coast of Indonesia, is about the size of most human fingernails at around 16mm (0.6in) long. Previously, experts had believed it to be the young of the next smallest seahorse species: *Hippocampus bargibanti*.

In a Nuclear Whirl

A seal went on a wild-water ride and in the process caused a nuclear alert in Britain in the 1990s. The seal, dubbed Lear, was sucked in with a massive water intake from the English Channel into the Dungeness nuclear power station and although weighing 136kg (300lb), she got through a security grille. In a torrent of water rushing in at 2.3 million litres (500,000 gallons) a minute, she was swept along a series of pipes and into a holding tank. Because of the whirlpool created in the tank, rescue by conventional diver or boat was impossible and so a crane was lowered into a diving platform with a net. Lear, however, was in no hurry and swam around for another 72 hours before she was rescued, unharmed.

Cat's Tailback

One of Britain's busiest roads was brought to a standstill in 2012 when a cat became trapped in an overhead sign gantry 15m (50ft) above the M4 motorway. A cherry picker truck had to be brought in and a rescuer lured the cat out of its hiding place with food. Despite its 24-hour high-rise stay on the gantry, it was unharmed.

Lemur High Life

It is almost unknown for the feet of the mouse lemur to touch the ground. The smallest primate in the world at 5–12cm (2–5in) rarely leaves the trees of the Madagascar forest. With these lemurs enjoying the high life, it is hardly surprising that they have only recently been identified, when they were immediately declared an endangered species because of the loss of their limited forest habitat.

Birds Top Air Travel

Egyptian geese beat aircraft to the higher layers of the Earth's atmosphere when a flock was photographed by an astronomer at the edge of the stratosphere – 8km (26,000ft) up – in 1919.

Wee Doggy

A frightened puppy put a dampener on one of England's most famous footballers in a 1962 World Cup match in Chile. The small dog had managed to get on the field of play between Brazil and England and it was English striker Jimmy Greaves who picked it up with a view to taking it off the field. But even the diminutive goal-scoring legend Greaves was too much for the pup and out of fear, it peed on his shirt. Rival winger Garrincha found the whole incident so funny he adopted the dog.

In the Pink

A kitten born amid the dust of a cement factory had a permanent pink coat. The tiny "Pink Panther" was rescued by animal charity workers from behind pallets in 2011 and although his siblings had natural-coloured coats, a harmless red dye at the factory in Redruth, Cornwall, England had stained Pink Panther's cream fur.

Short Stay

The world's smallest frog – the Monte Iberia Eleuth – was only discovered in the 21st century, but may not be around long enough for scientists to find out more about it. Discovered on a mountain in Cuba, and measuring just 8.5mm (0.33in), scientists declared it critically endangered.

Keep Hangin' On

A cat clung to a family's roof rack because it couldn't bear to be parted from them. The Humphreys' tabby cat Gato was discovered still hanging on for dear life after 160km (100 miles) when they stopped to catch a ferry at the Isle of Wight, England.

Foundation of a City

The city of Phalia in modern-day Pakistan is said have been built over the grave of Alexander the Great's horse, Bucephalus.

Supergrass Bird

One of the best early-warning systems in the animal world is the nutcracker. As its cry of "kre, kre, kre" spreads across the wildernesses of the USA, Canada and Mexico, other wildlife – furred and feathered alike – know danger is about. Hunters call the nutcracker the "informer bird".

Mini Record

At just 15cm (5.9in) tall, Mr Peebles was officially declared the World's Smallest Cat in 2012. A genetic defect that stunts growth meant that he was included in the *Guinness World Records*. Able to fit comfortably into a pint glass, the itsy-bitsy kitty was born in 2009, in Illinois, USA and owner Robin Svendson named her pet after a ventriloquist's dummy in the US sitcom *Seinfeld*. His best friends were Robert the guinea pig and the big German shepherd dog, Gravy.

Swanning Around

A royal swan was so long-lived that he saw in the reigns of four British monarchs. "Old Jack" was born in Buckingham Palace Gardens in 1770 and by the time he died in 1840, he had lived through part of the reign of George III, the whole reigns of George IV and William IV, as well as the first three years of Queen Victoria's monarchy.

Post Haste

A dog that was adopted by the US postal service in the 1880s ended up travelling 230,000km (143,000 miles) with the mail. Owney was a scruffy stray that wandered into the post office at Albany, New York and became fixated with accompanying the mail. He began travelling on mail trains and became a talisman for the service because no train he was on ever suffered an accident or was robbed. Owney became a firm favourite and a fixture throughout the system; workers even made him a special coat on which they fixed metal tags to denote where he had been. He spread his wings from mainland USA to Canada and Mexico before joining ships that were taking mail to the Middle East, the Azores and the Far East. His coat, bedecked with 1,017 tags, remains an exhibit at the Smithsonian Institute's Museum of American History in Washington DC.

Flying Messenger

An albatross became an unlikely carrier of messages during the days of the sailing ships in the later 19th century. In a bizarre turn of events, the crew of the British frigate *Duchess of Argyle*, off Cape Horn, captured an albatross and found it carried a case with a message in it from sailors aboard the US ship *Columbus* in 1850. The *Duchess of Argyle* crew wrote a new message and freed the bird (who was captured by a third ship, a few months later). This time they found that in the interim the bird had visited a fourth crew, this time of shipwrecked sailors, who had used it to send a plea for help. Unfortunately, by the time a rescue bid could be mounted, the crew on the southern tip of South America had already perished.

Hi, Shorty!

A Chihuahua called Ducky was officially named the World's Smallest Dog in 2007. At just 635g (1.4lb) and 12.4cm (4.9in) tall, Ducky was by no means the smallest adult dog ever recorded, however. That honour went to a dwarf Yorkshire terrier of 7cm (2.8in).

Long Commute

Scientists believe loggerhead turtles will go a long way for love. Those hatched in the Pacific Ocean off Japan migrate 10,400km (6,500 miles) to the west coast of the USA in search of a mate, then complete a round trip of 21,000km (13,000 miles) to nest.

Long Walkies Home!

When truck driver Geoff Hancock let his fox terrier out of his cab to stretch its legs, he didn't expect that it would be nine months before he saw him again. While Geoff took a coffee break in Darwin, Australia, Whisky got lost but eventually navigated his way to Hancock's home, some 2,900km (1,800 miles) away on the other side of the country in Melbourne.

Hard Seats

Birds in Britain can be a bit eccentric in their choice of material for building nests. A crow was once found to have built her nest entirely of barbed wire. In another bizarre discovery, a pigeon in Sheffield, Yorkshire had used long nails for its nest but added a few feathers for comfort.

Heroic Sefton

An army horse survived some of the most horrific injuries ever inflicted on an animal. Sefton was one of a troop of Blues and Royals Guards caught in a terrorist bomb blast in London, 1982. The 19-year-old was given no chance after his jugular vein was severed and there were 28 pieces of shrapnel found in his body; also, a 15cm (6in) nail had penetrated his leather bridle and become lodged in his head. However, with the amazing skills of veterinary surgeons, he managed to pull through and became a national hero.

Write On

In AD77, Roman author and naturalist Pliny the Elder claimed that he had witnessed a literate elephant that could write the phrase "I, the elephant, wrote this" in the sand with its trunk.

Match This For Size

A mini hamster that could fit in a matchbox was declared the world's smallest in 2003. Although an adult, Peewee measured less than an inch (2.4cm), weighed less than an ounce (28g), and looked like a newborn.

Forgetting to Duck

A duck interrupting a Finnish First Division football tie in 1993 failed to move "quackly" enough and was poleaxed by a corner kick. Medics revived the unconscious bird but it was soon well enough to fly away.

Grand Hero

Just weeks after almost drowning at sea, a horse won the demanding Grand National steeplechase in England. In 1904, it looked all over for Moifaa, a tough South African horse entered for the race, as he was fighting for his life in giant waves when the ship taking him to England sank in a storm. The gutsy horse stayed afloat and made it 160km (100 miles) back to South Africa – where, incredibly, his owners put him right back on another ship. After hearing of the horse's experience, the British race punters didn't rate his chances but Moifaa romped home the clear winner at 25-1.

Noisy Neighbour

Romanian police found a three-year-old lion in a man's backyard after a neighbour reported hearing a roar in 2003. They also discovered three deer and two peacocks – no doubt equally nervous about the lion neighbour.

Winning At a Gallop

One of the earliest recorded events of animals having a major impact on the outcome of a war is 1,650BC, when the nomadic Hyksos used single horses and crude chariots to conquer Egypt. But the Egyptians learned fast and in turn overthrew the Hyksos with better chariots powered by two horses.

Bird in a Million

A racing pigeon was sold for almost a million francs in 1975. An English enthusiast bought the bird from a Belgian owner for £12,075 ($19,150).

Beware, Low-Flying Cow!

A cow tried flying – not once but twice in her life. Fawn, a Guernsey cow, was living on a farm in the tornado-prone American state of Kansas when in 1962, a twister picked her up and she flew for more than 2.4km (1.5 miles) to a neighbouring farm. Five years later, a repeat experience saw her safely touch down after being "flown" over a bus to the other side of a road.

Monumental Mouser

Towser, a longhaired tortoiseshell, was declared a world record holder for catching 28,899 mice at the Glenturret Distillery, near Crieff in Perthshire, Scotland. Barley stored at the distillery, where the Famous Grouse brand was distilled, was a magnet for mice – but not while Towser was about, from 1963 until she died in 1987. Her exploits are commemorated by a bronze statue at Glenturret.

Horse Hero

Alexander the Great afforded his horse a soldier's burial with full military honours in 326BC. The Macedonian king had conquered most of the known world from the back of his horse, Bucephalus, over 30 years before the steed was fatally wounded in the Battle of the Hydaspes in what is now Pakistan.

Dead Expensive

Someone once paid £9,000 ($14,000) for... a dead bird! But the director of Iceland's Natural History Museum believed it was worth it in 1971 since this was one of the finest stuffed examples of the great auk, which had been extinct since 1844, and was one of the last remaining specimens in the world.

Puppy Love

$4,000 ($2,500) is quite a price to pay for a puppy. That's $1,000 per leg – unless the puppy is a five-legged one. Originally named Precious, the puppy, which had an extra leg growing out of her abdomen between her hind legs, was bought by Allyson Siegel to save her from the clutches of a freak show. The North Carolina woman with a heart of gold renamed the puppy Lilly and gave her a loving home. On another happy note, a Manhattan vet was so touched by Siegel's kindness that he offered to remove Lilly's extra leg for free.

Turtle Trek

A pet turtle called Byrtle decided to put some miles between himself and his owner in the 1990s. After absconding from his pen in Long Beach, California, it was 10 years before Byrtle was found – 320km (200 miles) inland.

Egg Record's No Yolk

A hen came up trumps when she was tested for egg output in 1930. The black Orpington, living in New Zealand, missed just three days' laying and had produced an incredible 361 eggs in 364 days.

Loony Depths

The common loon bird can reach superhuman depths in its search for food. Also known as the great northern diver, it plunges depths of 75m (240ft) when it dives into the lakes and rivers of the USA. All this at depths where for humans, oxygen becomes toxic and results in sensory distortions and seizures that can prove fatal.

Moving Mountains For Fish

Building a fishpond was a mountainous task for super-rich Roman politician Lucullus. In 50BC, his crew of workers cut through a mountain near Naples, Italy, to allow seawater to flow into the pond.

Slow Stroll

A tortoise that went missing for 35 years turned up just 600m (656 yards) from where he set out. His owner – Malcolm Edwards of Hertfordshire, England – was just eight years old when Chester went walkabout and was 43 by the time the tortoise had been recovered. Chester was recognized by the now-faded white cross that had been painted on his back, all those years before.

Polly-glots

Multi-lingual pals Ito and Jocotte stunned the parrot world in the 1960s by displaying a set of amazing language skills. The two parrots, owned by a French lawyer, each had a vocabulary of 500 words – some French, and some in English.

War Break

During a lull in the Great War in 1917, cavalry horses were given some recreation. Normally terrified by the sounds of war, they were treated to jumping competitions and even steeplechase courses were put up. The break in the war during May of that year was caused by unusually hot weather.

Crusty Crustacean

In 1974, a French restaurant owner was fined after a live lobster plucked from a tank for boiling got its revenge in first by snipping off part of a diner's nose! The police charged the restaurateur with failing to control a dangerous animal.

Boring Life

The larvae of the metallic wood-boring beetle surprised workmen by emerging alive in 1889 after being encased in a step at Copenhagen University Library, Denmark, in 1860.

Pigeon's Nine Lives

Forget cats, some pigeons have nine lives, too! A British Army messenger pigeon called Mary of Exeter won the highest animal honours for her catalogue of heroic achievements. She flew throughout the whole of World War II and survived some horrific injuries on the way, requiring 22 stitches. Just two months after having her neck and breast ripped open by a hawk attack, she fluttered in with a shot-away wing and her body riddled with pellets. She still wasn't safe because after being sent to Exeter for recuperation, the Germans followed her and a bomb landed close to her loft, which killed other pigeons but not Mary. More was to follow, as weeks later she was found more dead than alive in a field with head and body injuries. With the help of a special leather collar to hold her head up, she survived once more to win the Dickin Medal for bravery and earn retirement from military service.

Mane Event

The famous Roman general Mark Antony is credited with being the first person to have broken lions to a yoke and harnessed them to a chariot.

Fishy Tale

Although never officially authenticated because records then were sketchy, a pike fish had a claimed age of 267 years in the Middle Ages in Germany. It was caught in a lake in 1497 measuring 5.1m (15.9ft) and had a copper tag saying it had been placed in the waters in 1230.

Old Boy Koi!

A koi carp had lived for so long that it was tended by seven generations of the same family during the 20th century.

Horse Heroes Come Home

Horses used by the British Army on the battlefields of France were allowed to wear campaign medals on their bridles when they returned home after the Great War of 1914–18.

Cow With Udder Ideas

A desperate cow cruelly separated from her calf took matters into her own hands and hoofed it. Daisy lost her baby when she was sold at auction at Okehampton in Devon in the 1980s. But she escaped from her new home by jumping a gate and trekked 10km (6 miles) to her old home to be reunited with her offspring. Daisy's rebellious show of devotion made the reunion permanent as her new owner bought her calf, too.

Pampered Pony

Roman Emperor Caligula may have been a tyrant to humans, but he loved his horse Incitatus. As well as being attended by 18 servants, it was fed oats mixed with gold flake. Incitatus had a stable of marble with an ivory manger, purple blankets and a collar of precious stones. It was documented at the time – 39AD – that Caligula planned to make his equine friend a consul, a move that would have given the horse administrative, legislative and judicial powers.

Moving Story of Motherhood

A family who befriended a stray while on holiday in the 1990s had no idea that they would have six cats of their own inside six months. After their vacation in upstate New York, they returned to New York City a month later only to find the stray Daisy carrying a kitten in her mouth. Leaving it behind, she disappeared before, a month later, coming back with another baby. She repeated this three more times to complete her family in her adopted home.

Daytripper Dog

Most dogs use their four feet when they get the wanderlust but Spot, a Wales-based sheepdog, decided a National Express coach was easier. The eight-month-old pet hopped on a coach at Cardiff in 1983 and, having repelled with bared teeth any attempts to get him off, he rode all the way to London and then ran off. Half an hour later, he reappeared, took up his customary seat behind the driver and rode all the way back where the Royal Society for the Prevention of Cruelty to Animals (RSPCA) was waiting to reunite him with his family – a round trip of 400km (250 miles).

Raven Mad

A raven won roles in 200 Hollywood movies during the 1930s and 40s. Jimmy had an amazing array of tricks, such as operating a cash register, typing a letter and straightening a co-star's bow tie and pocket-handkerchief. The raven, which appeared in films such as Jimmy Stewart's *You Can't Take It With You*, could be light-fingered though, and also stole money and jewels.

Well Done At Verdun

A messenger dog played a heroic and vital part in turning the Battle of Verdun the Allies' way in 1916. Satan, a cross-greyhound with the French Army, managed – despite being riddled with gunfire – to deliver carrier pigeons in baskets to a French command centre. In doing so, he gave his life but one of the pigeons got a message through for artillery to be turned on a vital sector to wipe out a German gun battery, which it did successfully.

Full Marks to Harpo

A dog called Harpo came to the rescue of a three-year-old boy feared dead on the Spanish Balearic island of Menorca in 1983. Search parties failed to find Oscar Simonet and it was feared he might have fallen off a cliff-top near his village of Villacarlos and been swept out to sea – until Irish setter Harpo stepped in. The Mayor's pet pestered his master until he followed him to a cliff-top tangle of bushes. In a hidden metre-deep (3ft) crevasse, the Mayor found a semi-conscious but unharmed Oscar.

Papal Bull Elephant

One of the more bizarre tales of animalistic devotion throughout history was that of 16th-century Pope Leo X and his beloved white elephant, Hanno. It was said that the elephant wept with joy when it saw Leo and would go down on bended knee in salute. Even a purgative containing gold failed to save Hanno when the creature fell ill, but Leo X commissioned master painter and architect Raphael to eulogize the elephant with a painting above the animal's tomb in Rome.

Bit Snippy

There have been several instances in history when lobsters angry at being disturbed have snipped through a diver's snorkel tubes with their sharp claws. No doubt the divers would have headed for the surface as soon as possible after that.

Wiry Dogs

Dogs were used by the British Army to lay telegraph cable across vast areas of the Western Front during the Great War of 1914–18. Revolving drums of cable were strapped to breeds such as German shepherds and the dogs were sent running between two points to reel out the wire behind them as they went.

Cliff-hanger Dog Story

A faithful dog refused to leave his master's side – even after he fell 50m (164ft) down a cliff in Denmark. Farmer Alf With's fall in 1992 was broken by a ledge, otherwise he would have plunged further to certain death. Amazingly, Tony the red setter scrambled down and kept him warm for 16 hours until both were airlifted to safety after Alf's cries for help were heard by passers-by.

Chihuahua Chic

When the owner of pampered pooch Rocky reviewed his wardrobe in Kent, England, in 2012 he had 1,500 designer outfits worth an amazing £2,500 ($4,000).

Animal Spotter

The all-conquering army of Alexander the Great had a very
different role to play as they overwhelmed huge tracts of Europe
and Asia around 332BC – they were wildlife spotters. Previously
Alexander's teacher and mentor, the philosopher Aristotle, had
made his pupil passionate about natural history and Alexander
therefore ordered his men and new subjects to report on
anything of zoological interest. The information was sent
back to Aristotle, enabling him to write his *History of Animals.*

By George, I'm Lost!

In the 1990s the good name of St Bernards as mountain rescuers
was sullied by George, a dog who became lost in the Swiss Alps
looking for two climbers. The climbers were found by a separate
search party, which then had to go and look for gormless George.
It was the last straw and he was drummed out of the mountain
rescue organization because this was the eighth time in two years
that his nose and sense of direction had let him down.

Turning the Tables

Camels can be obstinate when being led where they do not want
to go but their natural tendency to pull backwards was used
against them by British troops in the desert war of World War
II, when trying to load them onto trains. The camel handlers
blindfolded the beasts and turned them around several times
until their backs were to the train. A yank in the forward meant
that the creatures' bloody-mindedness would automatically
kick in and they would back up – right into the train.

Where Eagles Dare

The people of Canada proved to be the best friends of America's iconic bald eagle when severe weather threatened the species in January 2010. Temperatures in Comox, British Columbia plunged to almost record lows, which meant the eagles in the area were unable to find food. Caring local families gathered fish and fed the birds to help them survive. Following this, the majestic eagle network went into full swing and word got around. Soon the area was swamped by dozens of grateful birds.

Animals In, Two By Two

One of the most spectacular animal parades recorded in history came in 312BC. In Alexandria, Egyptian ruler Ptolemy I led 24 chariots drawn by elephants ahead of a procession of pairs of lions, leopards, panthers, camels, antelopes, wild asses, ostriches, a bear, a giraffe and a rhinoceros.

Hairy Moment

In 2012, the life of a cat close to death was saved by vets, who removed two fur balls from its stomach at Huntingdon in England. The matted hair lumps were both the size of cricket balls – approximately 23cm (9in).

Grizzly Swim Companions

Guests head for the changing rooms at a Colorado hotel when certain visitors turn up for a swim. Grizzly bears have been known to come down from their mountain home to luxuriate in the warm waters of the five-star Ritz-Carlton's outdoor swimming pool.

Ranger's Wild Rapport

Like a modern-day Doctor Dolittle, wildlife ranger Kevin Richardson had developed an incredible bond with his charges in an African national park in 2011. He regularly swam and romped with lions, cuddled black panthers and enjoyed close-up rough-and-tumbles with wild dogs and hyenas – some of the bush's most vicious animals. This incredible interaction between man and many types of beast amazed scientists and other observers.

Florence's Feathered Friend

A tiny owl must have thought it had gone from the frying pan to the fire when it was rescued from being stoned by boys in Greece. Its saviour was Florence Nightingale, a young nurse, who put the feathered baby she named Athena into her pocket. She took it to the battlefields of the Crimean War in 1854, where Britain was fighting Russia. Florence was to become a national heroine in Britain by revolutionizing how wounded soldiers were nursed in war.

Beastly Swap

The first giraffe seen in Europe was in 1261 and came about as a result of a deal between monarchs. Fredrick II of the Two Sicilies took the long-necked beast from the Sultan of Egypt in exchange for a white bear.

Birds of Spray

A New Zealand farmer tried to fool tourists in 2012 into believing that he had discovered a new species of hawk by spraying brown ones red. His trick was found out, however, though none of the birds was harmed.

Leonar-doh!

Amazingly for a technological genius who conceptualized a helicopter, a tank, concentrated solar power and the calculator, Leonardo da Vinci believed in unicorns. He had a 15th-century theory that they could be captured by using a young woman as bait and the unicorn would be so overcome, it would sit in her lap. He even sketched the scenario.

Coral Tells the Time

21st-century scientists have learned from coral that the world has slowed down from a 400-day year to today's 365. That's because coral grows at a different rate during the night to the day and measurements showed that in 400 million years, the earth day has grown shorter by a second every 132 years.

Lobster Wrath

When captured, lobsters have been known to do strange things. Indeed one retaliated against a French fisherman in the 1950s by reportedly pulling the plug from the bottom of his boat. The man had to battle not only to save his boat but also his valuable catch.

Wily Coyote

Colliding with a car at 120kph (75mph) is usually fatal for a coyote but one tough creature survived not only that, but also a 965km (600 miles) journey jammed under the front bumper. In 2011, brother and sister Daniel and Tevyn East were driving at night near the Nevada-Utah border in the USA when they felt a bump. After deciding no animal could survive such an impact, they went on for another eight hours and 600 miles. Their arrival in California was the first chance to inspect the possibly gruesome damage and they were amazed to discover the coyote had survived despite being trapped under the front bumper.

Vital Deliveries

During World War II, dogs such as German shepherds were specially trained by the British Army to deliver drums of machine-gun ammunition to troops in those places inaccessible to vehicles.

Equine Air Rage

A plane flight in 2011 proved just too much for a highly-strung racehorse, which almost caused a crash. The horse panicked and terrorized aircrew on a flight from Mexico City to Long Beach, California by leaping about, frightening other horses and smashing down three barriers so that it was feared it would kick a hole in the fuselage. Luckily, the pilot managed to make an emergency landing, where a vet was standing by to sedate the scared animal.

Hamsters on the Rampage

Two escaped hamsters began a population explosion that turned into a plague for residents of an English suburb in 2011. The twosome started a family that multiplied to hundreds of wild hamsters – a species more at home in the wilds of the Middle East, Russia and Asia than a housing estate in Burnt Oak, north London. After the hamsters occupied local allotments, families had to block all possible entry points to their homes, including letterboxes and airbricks, because the little creatures flooded in and raided any food they could find. They also made scratching noises under floorboards and in attics that kept everyone awake. The local cats had a field day hunting them, but by 2011 the "gone native" hamsters were still breeding fast.

Elephant Memory

According to the saying, elephants never forget and this would seem particularly true of a family group in Zambia. Their ancestors always visited a certain area in the South Luangwa National Park when the fruit in a mango grove ripened. There was still no stopping them when one year the luxury Mfuwe Lodge was built close to the grove – the family simply followed their normal route and strolled through the lobby to reach their beloved bounty. Every November, hotel staff and visitors stand aside in awe as matriarch elephant Wonky Tusk leads her family up to four times a day to gorge on mangos for up to six weeks.

Lifesaving Bond

A dog saved from death by a man was eventually able to reciprocate. In the 1990s, Wilhelm Stachovski came to the rescue of Bruno who was being battered by a gang of thugs in Germany. Afterwards he nursed the dog back to health and adopted him. Some years later Bruno ran to a local café and dragged the proprietor by his clothes back to Wilhelm's house, where his owner was suffering a heart attack. His timely action meant an ambulance was called and Wilhelm's life was saved.

Dog Deserter

A harsh punishment usually awaits wartime deserters, though not a homesick guard dog in World War II. The chien de Brie was commandeered from his French home at the start of the war but all the army training in the world could not make him forget his traditional role of herding sheep and so he ran 500km (300 miles) back to the Avignon home he longed for. But there was no punishment for this particular deserter as the French Army decided that he had already served his time and had earned the reunion.

Clammy Feeling

Over the centuries, the shells of giant clams became prized baths for the emperors and court officials of China. Shells big enough to bathe in took more than 100 years to grow!

Saved By an Angel

A golden retriever literally threw itself into the jaws of death to save a young playmate. In 2010, Austin Forman, 11, was gathering firewood in his backyard in Boston Bar, British Columbia when seemingly for no reason 18-month-old dog Angel ran toward him, jumping over a lawn mower – right into the path of a charging cougar of which Austin had been unaware. When police arrived at the scene, they found Angel with the cougar's jaws gripped firmly round her neck. The big cat was shot dead but Angel came through the terrifying ordeal to make a full recovery despite extensive injuries, including a fractured skull.

Trunk Tricks

Waving a flag and firing a pistol were amazing tricks performed by female elephant Hanksen as she toured Europe with a circus in the 17th century. She could also beat a drum, steal money from pockets, put on a hat, carry a bucket of water and pick up coins.

Lost Record

A poodle died unfulfilled in 2012 because his American owners felt that he should have had a place in the *Guinness World Records*. Uncle Chichi was believed to be 26 years old but his birth records had been lost. This meant for the time being, the Guinness record stayed with a Japanese dog which had died only a month before.

Pulling Power

During the Great War, dog teams were used in the Alps to pull supplies and ammunition through places the horses couldn't get to. The Italian soldiers loved the dogs so much that they rewarded them with a tasty menu of coffee, bread, broth, meat, sugar and chocolate.

Comeback Kings

A species of monkey came back from the dead in 2011. The Miller's grizzled langur was thought to be extinct – until they turned up very much alive on camera. Scientists working in the jungle of Indonesia rediscovered the large grey monkey species by mistake as the cameras had been set up to capture images of cloud leopards and orang-utans. Because of a lack of earlier photographs, the langurs were confirmed through museum sketches.

Trixie's a Saviour

Drinking water from a dog's bowl and a toilet may have some "yuck!" value but it proved a lifesaver for Jack Fyfe when he had a paralysing stroke at his home in Western Australia. With uncanny prescience, his sheepdog Trixie seemed to know the one thing immobile Jack needed to sustain him was water. She grabbed a towel and soaked it in her own water bowl, then dropped in onto his face so that he could suck it. When her bowl was empty, she improvized with water from the toilet and for nine days kept Jack alive until relatives turned up and got him to hospital.

Canine Paratrooper

A collie-cross known as Rob was awarded the equivalent of Britain's Victoria Cross for making 20 jumps with the Parachute Regiment and the Special Air Service during World War II. He was awarded the Dickin Medal, the highest honour in Britain for animal bravery during dangerous work, including drops into North Africa and Italy.

Oscar Star Escapes Death

A dog actor who won huge acclaim in 2012 was once just days from death in an American dog pound, it was revealed. Uggie the Jack Russell was one of the film sensations of the year following his performance in the Oscar-winning silent movie *The Artist*, in which he appeared wearing a bow tie and stood on his hind legs and played dead. Owner Omar von Muller revealed that he had adopted Uggie from a Los Angeles home for strays just days before he was due to be put down. Uggie and *The Artist* also won Golden Globes, BAFTAs and an award at the Cannes Film Festival.

Bee Power

Angry bees don't give up easily and to prove it, they handed a man a world record in 1962. Johannes Relleke was attacked by wild bees at the Kamativi tin mine in Zimbabwe and was forced to jump into a nearby river. There he stayed for four hours during the sustained flying assault. Still exposed, his head was black with stings by the time he was rescued. Johannes survived but had more than 2,000 stings taken out of his face alone and a world record of 2,443 overall.

Off-air

An over-zealous guard dog did something storm, war and terrorism have all failed to do: silence the BBC. During World War II, the dog charged with guarding a radio station was let loose to tackle what was thought to be an intruder. It drove him halfway up a pylon but unfortunately it turned out to be an announcer taking a quick break from transmission. Left with dead air, the BBC were forced to apologize for a "technical hitch".

Great Esc-ape

Primates showed themselves capable of precision organization when they arranged a mass breakout from an English safari park in 1974. It seems the monkey population had been watching the iconic film, *The Great Escape*, because they sneaked past the tight security measures and clung to the underside of tourist buses at the park near Chester-le-Street, Co. Durham. The plot was foiled and the ringleaders identified. Their punishment was to be dispersed to other safari parks and zoos.

Bitsy's Love Bite

You'd think the last thing you would want if you were having a heart attack was for your own dog to bite you – but it saved the life of elderly Jesus Martinez in Houston, Texas in the 1990s. Schnauzer Bitsy literally leapt into action when he had a heart attack at the wheel of his car. Jumping into the driving seat, she knocked the wheel in the direction of the hard shoulder. She then bit her owner's leg until he lifted his foot off the accelerator and the car ground to a halt. Jesus recovered in hospital.

Apeing Humans

The first ape to be introduced to the public in London in the early 19th century was a male chimpanzee named Tommy, who was wearing a sailor suit. He was soon followed by Jenny, a female orang-utan wearing a dress. Both primates were taught to eat with spoons.

Chest in Time

Matthew Cook thought his new first-aid training would be used on humans, but it saved the life of his pet hamster Kimmie. The 15-year-old, who had just been awarded St John Ambulance first-aid certificates, found his pet apparently lifeless in its cage and performed chest massage on it until it breathed again.

Bob's Good Job

A mongrel dog called Bob saved a World War II British Army patrol from capture or death in 1943 – by freezing. On patrol during the North African campaign with C Company of the 6th Queen's Own Royal West Kent Regiment, the dog suddenly stopped in his tracks, silent and watchful. Seeing nothing ahead, the patrol was just about to move on when enemy lines were sighted. The British patrol retreated with invaluable information about enemy positions and owed their lives to Bob's sharp senses.

Neighbourly Newfoundland

Staffordshire bull terrier Mo believes Newfoundland bitch Molly is a fine neighbour. The enormous Newfoundland became a lifesaver when Mo ate rat poison and was given 24 hours to live unless a blood donor could be found. Molly is Mo's neighbour in the Somerset village of Bruton and at around 50kg (110lb) was thought to be big enough to give a pint of lifesaving blood. Two days after the donation, Mo had recovered sufficiently to go home and Molly suffered no ill effects.

Into the Light

A beetle emerged alive from a concrete grave after 16 years. The aptly named burying beetle had become embedded in the concrete.

Half-Hearted Escape

The escape plan of a group of hamsters got a bit distracted… by a mountain of food. Twenty-two of them escaped from their cage in a pet shop in Maesteg, South Wales, in 1989. But they made it only to a neighbouring greengrocer's store, where they gorged themselves, curled up and were caught napping.

Fin-tastic Lifesaver

One of the most incredible sights greeted rescuers after a tropical cyclone ravaged the Bangladeshi coast in 1991 – a dolphin with a tiny baby in its mouth. The youngster had been swept out to sea by the storm and the dolphin rescued it and held it safely out of the water, allowing rescuers to take it on board. Humanitarian job done, it simply swam away.

Crafty Monkeys

A group of troublesome baboons came up with a cunning plan to escape from a zoo in Amsterdam in 1984. With bananas, they lured an antelope sharing their enclosure into place alongside a fence and then used its back to make a vault for freedom. Eventually, they were recaptured but observers of the ploy were given a new insight into baboon behaviour.

Hair-raising Heroism

A labrador trapped in an upturned boat had more than just self-survival in mind as she escaped. Instead of striking out for the bank, Bo's first thought was for her owner Laurie Roberts, who was still trapped. She dived down again and pulled Laurie free by her hair. In the 1892 incident on a raging Colorado River in the USA, Bo's puppy Duchess also survived after being thrown out of the boat by a 2.4m (8ft) wave.

Tree-mendous Courage

A bad landing did not stop a World War II hero dog. Bing may have been a German shepherd but his heart was all-British as he landed with paratroopers in the first wave of the D-Day landings in 1944; his chute was snagged high in a tree and he had to endure a night's shelling before being rescued. Although sporting a neck injury, Bing eschewed treatment and took up his guard dog duties with front-line troops, ever on the alert for the enemy.

No Panic!

A tapir, freed when bush fires threatened the private California zoo where he lived, didn't panic. He just dived into the swimming pool at legendary publisher William Randolf Hearst's home, where he chilled out until the danger had passed. Meanwhile, the other animals at Hearst Castle had high-tailed it and needed to be rounded up.

Can't Bear the Heat

Australians witnessed the poignant sight of koala bears begging for water from humans. The exceptionally hot summer of 2008 saw temperatures soar to 50°C (120° Fahrenheit). For a week it was too hot for the native koalas, who were given water by caring people.

Eager Beavers

Beavers, which are not traditionally known to climb, still went "over the wall" to escape from Edinburgh Zoo in Scotland in the 1990s. The scheming beaver band built an extra-large lodge next to the wall of their enclosure and then used it as a ramp.

Quacking the Ice

Firemen had to be called to rescue a swan and a duck that had been frozen solid on a lake in Sunderland, England in 2012.

Houdini Eagle

Usually, it's traffic problems that bring London to a standstill, but in 1965 it was a golden eagle named Goldie. He escaped from London Zoo and traffic ground to a standstill as people stopped to watch the magnificence of Goldie soaring over Regent's Park on his 2m (6′6″) wingspan. The escape lasted 10 days before Goldie fell for a carefully-laid trap using a dead rabbit. Ten months later Goldie escaped again but it didn't get the vast media coverage and was short-lived.

Shell Saviour

A giant turtle came to the rescue of a South Korean sailor who fell overboard in the Bay of Bengal. Lom Yang-Yong grabbed the turtle, which kept him afloat for six hours until his ship found him. The pair were craned aboard and the turtle freed after a huge meal of meat and bananas.

Cowardly or Clever?

Things looked bad for a guard-dog who ran off as the enemy approached stealthily by night. The question was, had Sorter the war dog turned yellow? And the answer turned out to be no. While his fellow dogs attacked invading Athenians during the Peloponnesian war of 431–404BC, Sorter ran to awaken the sleeping Corinthians and mustered them just in time to charge to victory and save the day. Later, in Corinth the people erected a monument to the saviour inscribed: "Sorter, defender and saviour of Corinth".

Run Like the Wind!

Hurricanes aren't always a bad thing! The devastating 1992 storm that struck Florida meant freedom for thousands of animals in zoos and wildlife parks. With their fences and enclosures devastated, the animals, which included deer, snakes, lizards, pumas, wallabies, apes and lemurs, seized their liberty. The Florida wildlife scene has been altered because most of the escapees were never recaptured and have subsequently bred in the wild.

Avian News

The wider world got to know about Julius Caesar's conquest of Gaul and Wellington's victory at Waterloo by the same method – homing pigeons carrying the good news messages – unless you were French, of course.

Concrete Munch

Termites cost the local council in Darwin, Australia thousands of dollars in 1951. The little creatures had munched their way through the floor of the new council chamber.

Facing Adversity

Mine-sniffing dog Ricky didn't let a mine exploding less than a metre away stop him. Although injured in the face, he continued his work with the combat engineers identifying mines hidden on a canal bank in The Netherlands during World War II. For this, he was awarded the Dickin Medal, Britain's highest recognition of animal bravery.

Strong Stuff

In the 1970s, an orang-utan called Bob was matched in a weightlifting competition against a former Mr Universe at San Diego, California. The orang-utan easily won with a lift of over 226kg (498lb).

Big Cat Dig

An archaeological dig in 1930 unearthed from beneath the Tower of London in England the skulls of two lions and one leopard. They were thought to be part of the "lion tower" built by King Edward I in 1276.

Jumbo Drug Problem

In the 1990s, unscrupulous timber poachers in Thailand fed elephants amphetamines to speed up their illicit trade and many of the animals became addicted. Elephants could lift stolen logs more quietly than heavy machinery and this led to a massive rise in Thailand's zoos and vets finding elephants suffering from anorexia, hypertension, blurred vision and gastric ulcers – all side effects of long-term amphetamine use.

Short-lived Freedom

The first time off the lead was dramatic for Springer spaniel pup Woody in 2011. He tumbled 60m (200ft) from a cliff in Exmouth, Devon but only suffered cuts.

Mine's a Record

Soviet Army mine detecting dog Zucha sniffed out a record 2,000 mines in just 18 days during World War II.

Hero Turtle

Rescuers gave up hope of seeing any more survivors from a ferry fire and sinking in 1992 until a woman was seen hanging onto a giant turtle. Candelaria Villanueva was on the verge of giving up after 12 hours in the water when the turtle swam underneath her and lifted her up. A second, smaller turtle climbed onto Candelaria's back and gently bit her when she dozed off and was in danger of slipping off the giant shell.

Skyscraper Cat-astrophe

Curiosity almost killed a cat called Walter. Living high in a New York skyscraper block is not ideal for checking out what the window cleaner is doing. He slipped from a balcony and fell an incredible 18 floors into a lifesaving and fall-breaking bush. Afterwards, eye witnesses saw a dazed Walter calmly walk back into the apartment block and take a lift to his home.

Mine Choices

After finding dogs unsuitable for the task, over the years the US Army has tried to find an animal with the best mine-detecting skills. Choices have included pigs, coyotes, cats, racoons, skunks, deer and ferrets. Experiments proved pigs had the most potential, but a soldier walking a pig would have had an image problem.

Hopping It

A Swedish space experiment with frogs failed to get off the ground. In 1989, the Swedes were planning to establish if frogs were able to mate in the weightless conditions, but the frogs preferred the lily pad to the launch pad. Somewhat mysteriously, they disappeared on the way to the rocket that was to take them into space.

Was Goldilocks Real?

The children's nursery story, Goldilocks and the Three Bears, may have happened for real in the late 20th century in the former Yugoslavia. A lost five-year-old girl, when rescued, told how she had been befriended by three bears with whom she played and who had kept her warm at night.

Dogs of War

Two dogs almost caused an international incident in 1900. The German Kaiser Wilhelm II's ferocious dachshunds, Wadl and Hexl, killed one of the Austro-Hungarian Crown Prince's priceless golden pheasants on a visit to Archduke Franz Ferdinand's castle, in what is now the Czech Republic.

Russian Around

Playful crows have caused damage to one of the most iconic buildings in the world. The gold onion-shaped cupolas of the Moscow Kremlin provide an irresistible slide for crows but their claws have been scraping away at the gold. City officials tried playing the sound of frightened crows to deter them but the delinquent birds took no notice.

Flying Mail

The first recorded use of pigeons being employed to carry military messages was in 1,150BC, when the Sultan of Baghdad had notes on papyrus sheets strapped to the legs or the tail feathers of birds.

Bob-bing Away

Bob the orang-utan's constant escape attempts had become a real problem for his keepers at San Diego Zoo in California. Houdini Bob's exploits started on the evening of his arrival, when he was caught unravelling the wire to his cage. Moving him to a stronger one didn't prove any more successful because he managed to get through another mesh and was found in the penguins' pool. For years afterwards, he kept his keepers on their toes by dismantling cages.

Winging It

One of the greatest insect migrations ever witnessed was in 1928, when a flight of pale form butterflies took three months to pass over a wide area of east Africa.

Bear-ly Legal

The trial of a brown bear accused of terrorizing the inhabitants of a German village in 1499 was halted on a technicality. A wily advocate for the bear pointed out that under the laws of the time, the bruin was entitled to be tried by a jury of his peers. The case was ultimately dismissed because no one wanted the job of rounding up 12 other brown bears!

Tall Story

A giraffe caught the French public's imagination in 1824 when hundreds of thousands of people turned out to see her. The long-necked female, only the third seen in Europe, was a gift from Mehmet Ali Pasha, the Ottoman viceroy of Egypt to King Charles X of France. She was transported to Marseille on a ship that had to have a hole cut through the deck to accommodate her neck and then set forth on a 900km (560 mile) walk to Paris. The giraffe was a spectacle across France and in Paris, some 100,000 spectators lined the streets to see her dressed in a yellow coat and shoes. She died in Paris, some 18 years later, but was stuffed and displayed in the foyer of the Jardin des Plantes before being transferred to a museum at La Rochelle, where she remains.

Waved Goodbye

A mongrel dog called John swept away by a 16m (52ft) tsunami turned up at its home on the Japanese island of Okushiri, a year later. Its owners had no idea where it had been taken by the wave but John had developed an appetite for fish, which he had not had before.

Flying Saviours

Pigeons were credited with aiding Paris during the city's siege of 1870. Hundreds of thousands of messages were secured to the birds and flown out to allies over the heads of the besieging Prussian army. The pigeon squadron carried 150,000 official letters and an estimated million items of private correspondence. One bird alone was credited with carrying 40,000 letters.

Brownie Back From the Dead

A family dog became a very-much-alive "ghost". Brownie
the mongrel was hit by a car on the driveway of the Bratcher
family's New Mexico home and pronounced dead in 2011.
He was buried in a field despite three-year-old Toby Bratcher
maintaining he was still alive. The next day Brownie emerged
from his coma and burial alive and was seen sitting, tail
wagging, on the doorstep when the family came back
from a trip.

Dolphin Guides

Trust in dolphins saved the crew of a fishing boat off South
Africa in 1978. Lost in a dense fogbank, the crew saw their
vessel surrounded by dolphins and the skipper, regarding
it as an omen, changed course away from a treacherous
reef. He continued to follow the dolphin school and when
the fog lifted, the crew was amazed to discover they were
back in their home port.

Sweet Success

A pet dog displayed intelligence above expectation to save
her diabetic owner's life. Holly the West Highland terrier acted
quickly when Roz Brown collapsed. She grabbed a bag of jelly
babies, having seen Roz reach for them for an emergency sugar
rush in the past. Finding her owner unconscious, the dog
nuzzled the back of her neck until she was conscious and
able to take the lifesaving sweet.

Spooky Reunion

Christine Rowe thought she knew the dog behind bars that was howling at her in a California dog pound. Amazingly, it was her German shepherd Spook, whom she had last seen seven months and many hundreds of miles away after he fell overboard from a Canadian ferry. She had given Spook up for dead when he fell from the ship, off the British Columbia coast. Christine was relocating to Alaska when the tragedy happened and was only in Sacramento, California to visit relatives. Plucky Spook not only survived the icy Pacific Ocean off Canada but also made his way 1,200km (744 miles) to his former home.

Bravery Rewarded

The French Army rewarded carrier pigeons for their bravery with the Croix de Guerre but because a medal couldn't be pinned to their breasts, a ring bearing the same colours was fixed to their legs.

Bear-faced Cheek

An American family who built a playground complete with slides and swings for their three- and four-year-old sons found some unwelcome visitors had taken over within hours. They woke up the day after completing the new play centre at Milford, New Hampshire to find a family of bears playing happily on the equipment.

Super-Sized Spiders

The famous 19th-century British naturalist Henry Bates recorded seeing in South America a tarantula so large that children tied a string about its middle and led it around like a dog.

War Bear

During World War II, the Polish Army officially enlisted an orphaned bear named Wojtek. Troops serving in the Middle East swapped the bear for a few cans of meat. As he was used to carrying mortar shells in battle, he was given a name, rank and serial number in order to travel to theatres of war in Iraq, Syria, Palestine, Egypt and southern Italy. The bear was fed with fruits, marmalade, honey and syrup, and was often rewarded with beer.

High-speed Help

A pigeon had to fly at an incredible mile a minute to save the crew of a downed seaplane in the North Sea, off eastern England in 1918. They released the bird with an SOS plea and its flight time of 22 miles in 22 minutes was crucial: help arrived just as the craft was breaking up in heavy seas.

Getting a Lift

Animal-loving British soldiers refused to leave behind calves born on long desert journeys by camel during World War II. Instead they fashioned nets and folded the long-legged babies into them to be carried for up to six hours until the next rest stop, when they were allowed to scamper about.

Right Wrong Number

An amazing misdial reunited a pet falcon with his owner Harry Walker. Lenny the falcon had escaped from his home in Belper, England in 2009 so Harry rang the police but, by an amazing coincidence he misdialled the number, and instead got a family who said that Lenny was at that very moment perched on their fence!

Lobster Saviour

Wealthy Saudi Sheik Mohammed al-Fassi was renowned for going into restaurants around the world and buying up every live lobster destined for the pot and the dinner table and releasing them back into their natural habitat.

Tanks For the Cash

Tanks on manoeuvres gave a farmer an idea for a moneymaking scam that duped the US military in 1942. The famous General George Patton's tank regiment passed by a Tennessee farm but a herd of goats keeled over at the noise and clanking of tracks. Following his loss, the farmer sued the military and won compensation – and also had the last laugh. His herd was of fainting goats, which keel over if startled. Not long after the tank convoy had gone, the "dead" goats were back on their feet. The Germans were no match for Patton during World War II but the General was equally outmanoeuvred by a simple farmer.

Dolphin-powered Dinghy

After abandoning his crashed helicopter in the Pacific Ocean, a pilot had his dinghy pushed by a dolphin for nine days. As soon as land was sighted, the kind-hearted mammal left his side.

What a Hero!

Woodie the mongrel was voted America's Dog Hero of the Year in 2002 after an amazing rescue that involved a 24m (80ft) leap from a cliff. He was walking in the Rock River reservation in Ohio with his owner Ray Thomas. While taking a photograph of a spectacular view, Ray fell off a cliff. He ended up unconscious in a fast-flowing river so Woodie leapt after him and despite breaking both hips in the plunge, kept nudging Ray's head above the water until help arrived. Both Ray and Woodie made a full recovery.

Banking On a New Life

A Dutch bank found itself with some strange "assets" when a fur farm went bust. It was left owning 850 coypus and although destroying them was discussed, animal protection societies persuaded the bank to repatriate the animals to their native South America so they got an all-expenses paid air trip to Uruguay – and freedom.

Hero Cat Broke Into Jail

There is a small memorial tucked away in a village church in Kent, England dedicated to a cat that broke into the Tower of London to save a prisoner. Sir Henry Wyatt was left to starve as a political prisoner in 1483. Expected to last only weeks, Wyatt lived on for month after month, his cause having been taken up by a stray cat, which slept with him at night and provided him with warmth. By day the cat hunted pigeons for him to eat and he survived long enough to be freed when his ally Henry VII was secure on the throne. So grateful was Wyatt that he had the memorial erected in Boxley church.

Counter Espionage

During World War II, carrier pigeons were used as a counter espionage ploy. As pigeons didn't wear uniforms or insignia, it was never clear whose side they were on and so the difference was in the construction of the message carrier. The Germans put some typically Teutonic "Vorsprung durch Technik" into a more elaborate model while the English version was plain. All it took was for a craftsman to copy the German ones, which were sent back to the war zone with misleading messages.

Arise, Sir Nils

A penguin went from "emperor" to "sir" in 2008. Nils Olav was knighted for long-time service as the mascot of the Norwegian King's Guard. In the formal ceremony, Nils – an emperor penguin – waddled through and made to inspect rows of soldiers before having the King's sword touched on both flippers.

Watch Out, Picasso!

An earthworm became the richest on record when it earned thousands of dollars as a painter. Between 1963–65 Willie the worm, who was based in the USA, churned out 200 works of art, which found buyers. He was dipped in harmless paint and wriggled his way across the canvas. When one colour was finished, he was dipped in another and set to work again. After two years, he was retired.

Dog Wants Boney

History has not portrayed Napoleon Bonaparte as a man given to emotion but it took a heartbroken dog to show the French dictator's softer side. After the battle of Marengo in Italy, in 1800, a dog spent hours tried to rouse his dead master and then ran to Bonaparte himself. The dog reduced Bonaparte to tears and spurred him on to write about the incident in his memoirs.

Putin Him to Sleep

In 2008, the undoubted gun skills of Russian President Vladimir Putin came into play when he was visiting a Siberian wildlife reserve to observe how tigers are monitored. An Ussuri tiger escaped from its restraints and threatened the visiting party but before the tiger could do any damage, action man Putin intervened and shot it with a tranquilizer gun.

The Ultimate in Recycling

When times get hard for the ever-hungry ribbon worm they become self-sufficient – literally. Usually they feed voraciously on dead animals but when there is nothing else to munch on, they eat themselves. They have the ability to sustain themselves by eating up to 95 per cent of their own bodies and when food is plentiful again, they grow back to their former size.

Caring Elephant

An elephant working in India showed amazing compassion and intelligence in the 1920s. Chandraskharan's task was to lift a huge wooden pillar into a hole in the ground, but he suddenly refused to do so because a dog had fallen asleep in the pit. Only when workers shooed the dog to safety did the elephant complete his task.

Buffon Buffoonery

Locals were up in arms when French naturalist Comte de Buffon criticized the climate of North America and asserted the country would have had almost no large mammals in 1787. His remarks particularly incensed US founding father Thomas Jefferson, who ordered a search of the New Hampshire woods for the biggest bull-moose as proof of the "stature and majesty of American quadrupeds".

Binge-drinking Elephants

A herd of some 150 elephants came across an illegal liquor stall in 1974 and drank the place dry. Afterwards they went on a drunken rampage through a West Bengal village, crushing homes and injuring residents in their wake.

Horse Find

A species of tiny horse only seen in ancient cave paintings was spotted for the first time by a scientific expedition in the Riwoche Valley of Tibet. They stumbled upon the undiscovered breed of horse by accident and found they were still in widespread use among locals.

Shy Shark

The frilled shark has rarely been viewed alive because its natural habitat is up to 304m (1,000ft) underwater – deeper than humans can dive. It has been dubbed a "living fossil" because scientists have dated the species back to 800 million years ago.

Bear Siege

Thirty hungry bears laid siege to a team of geologists in the Russian far-eastern region of Kamchatka. The scientists were trapped in their survey site for several days in 2008 because they did not have permission to shoot the bears so they had to wait until the bruins got bored and wandered off into the forest.

What a Girl!

German shepherd dog Girl was the right girl in a desperate situation as her owner, Ray Ellis, found out in 1985 because he lived to tell the tale. He was cutting firewood with a chainsaw when a branch fell and knocked him unconscious. Added to that, the chainsaw fell and severely injured his leg. Seeing that Ray was bleeding profusely, Girl ran a quarter of a mile to raise the alarm with Ray's wife. Thankfully, help arrived before he bled to death and he went on to make a full recovery.

Ray of Success

A stingray, which measured 5m (16ft 6in) in width, is believed to be one of the largest ever caught. In 2008, the 1,496kg (3,298lb) giant was captured off the coast of eastern China.

Coming By Return

Bad planning foiled thieves who stole 62 homing pigeons from a loft in Lancashire, England. But they had reckoned without the "homing" part of the pigeons' nature and within days, owner John Ashcroft had all bar 19 birds safely back home.

Winkie the Wonder Bird

In 1942, a blue chequered pigeon called Winkie beat all the odds to save an aircraft crew. It was normal for a carrier pigeon to be carried by aircrew in World War II so that if the aircraft got in trouble, the pigeon could carry an SOS to its base. However, more things than usual went wrong for the crew of a Beaufort fighter crew ditching in the North Sea, off Scotland. Winkie was thrown loose rather than released and her feathers became clogged in oil from the plane's engines. Dazed but unhurt, she followed her instinct and set off for home – 208km (129 miles) away – with no message attached. Fortunately the base commander put two and two together and realized his crew were somewhere in the North Sea in a dinghy. Thanks to Winkie's courage, they were soon rescued.

Cat Freaks

Around 940BC everyone was crazy about cats in the Egyptian city of Bubastis. So crazy, in fact, that they built a metropolis of worship for the feline-goddess Bast and with large parts of the city dedicated to her, cats were revered by a whole population. In 1888, an Egyptian farmer accidentally discovered a large tomb hosting tens of thousands of mummified cats!

Thirsty Work

A quick sip is not enough for vampire bats, who feed on animal blood. Once they have latched onto their victim, they keep sucking until their bodies have bloated into a round furry ball. Altogether, they steal 27 litres (46 pints) from their victims in a year.

Leo Loved Big Cats

Sixteenth-century Pope Leo X had an extensive menagerie in the Vatican and brought with him tigers, civet cats, leopards, bears and monkeys. The tigers were fed cooked meat because Leo believed it kept them from developing a taste for human blood. He also imported Renaissance Rome's first chameleon for his zoo.

Sausages For Hearst

There was only one breed of dog to really delight US newspaper magnate William Randolf Hearst – dachshunds. He had as many as 70 "sausage" dogs in kennels at his castle in San Simeon, Califronia in the 1920s. When one of his favourites (Helena) died, he eulogized her across a vast media empire in his "In the News" column.

Turkey Trot

A mysterious wild turkey has taken up residence in New York's Battery Park since mid-2003. She seemed to prefer to move in one direction because all subsequent sightings of the illusive Zelda have been increasingly south. In 2004, she ventured out of the park to Tribeca before being captured and returned to Battery Park. Thank goodness it wasn't Thanksgiving Day, when the USA traditionally eats turkey!

Pig is a Lottery Winner

Liz Kaernestam was prepared to put her money where her conscience was to save a piglet. The Austrian animal lover read that a Hungarian lottery was offering a piglet as a first prize and to save it from someone else's oven, she bought every ticket. Needless to say, she won!

Wings of Speed

A rapid flight by a pigeon serving in World War II prevented a "friendly fire" incident that might have caused many deaths. During the Italian campaign in 1943, a British infantry division called for air support in assaulting a German stronghold. The US aircraft were only seconds from taking off when pigeon GI Joe arrived after a 100kph (62mph) flight to stop them because the stronghold had fallen to the British. If Joe hadn't arrived then, the Americans would have been bombing British troops.

Michael's Animal Fans

Late pop superstar Michael Jackson's Neverland Ranch in California featured a zoo with giraffes, elephants, snakes, orang-utans, tigers and crocodiles. Jackson's favourite was a chimpanzee called Bubbles which he adopted from a Texas research facility in the early 1980s. Jackson even took Bubbles to Japan where he caused a stir by taking the chimp to tea with a mayor.

Making a Break For It

Reggie, an alligator thought to have been raised in illegal captivity, went feral in 2007 and took up residence in a lake in South Bay, Los Angeles. The legendary Australian crocodile hunter Steve Irwin died before he could carry out a pledge to catch Reggie, but the gater was later caught and given a permanent home Los Angeles Zoo.

Wolves Save Girl

In a tale resembling that of Roman twin brothers Romulus and Remus, a pack of wolves in Azerbaijan adopted a girl of three and protected her until rescuers turned up. Mekhriban Ibagimov was lost in woods in 2003 for several days but had been taken under the wing of a wolf pack, who kept her warm during the cold nights. Rescuers found Mekhriban snuggled up to a she-wolf.

Hearty Effort

Animal lover Ursula Herberger used cardiac massage to save the life of a baby rabbit that she found while walking in Switzerland.

Ewe Hero You!

A cross-species love affair was a lifesaver for one of the partners on a farm in Northumberland, England in 1984. Gilbert the goose, who had lost his mate, found a new friend in a pregnant ewe and slavishly followed her everywhere. When the expectant mum collapsed with complications connected with her pregnancy, Gilbert went berserk and flapped around, honking loudly, until farmhands came to see what the racket was. They provided timely help to save both the sheep and her lamb.

Remembered in Bronze

A bronze statue of an akito dog stands at Tokyo's Shibuya Station as testament to a dog's unwavering loyalty to his master, even beyond the grave. The statue is dedicated to Hachiko, who in the mid-1920s belonged to a professor in the agriculture department at the University of Tokyo. Every morning, the dog saw his master off at the front step and then waited at the railway station when he was due to return. In 1925, the professor died of a brain haemorrhage and never came home. Hachiko waited at the station until midnight and then returned the next day, when he waited again. He did so every day for 11 years until his death in 1934. Commuters were so touched that a bronze statue was erected in Hachiko's memory.

Amazing Monkey Farmer

Johnnie Schmidt was an exceptional farmhand. For nine years from 1956, he worked for six days a week, 12 hours a day driving a tractor, delivering hay and opening and shutting gates. Not bad for a rhesus monkey adopted by Australian farmer Lindsay Schmidt at three weeks old. Johnnie also lived like a human: wearing workgear and cardigans, cleaning his teeth and even taking baths.

Baywatch Saves Bunny

James Thorogood had no medical or first-aid training but he saved the life of his pet rabbit Boogedy with an artificial respiration method learned from watching the hit TV series, *Baywatch*. Boogedy had been pulled unconscious from the swimming pool at James's home in Australia.

Boris is a Bruiser

In 2003, a domesticated badger named Boris got grumpy and went on a two-day rampage in England. He attacked five people and two police officers trying to capture him were forced to run for the safety of their patrol car.

Whale Strikes a Chord

Recordings of Vivaldi and Chopin played underwater helped a whale back to the sea in 1993. Stranded for days in a German port, it had become confused about its way out. Playing the classical music masters calmed the whale enough for it to be guided back to safety.

Cat Guts

A mystery cat became a 2012 internet hit after a gutsy fight with an alligator. The two had an on-camera stand-off over chicken meat at the Cajun Pride swamp in LaPlace, Louisiana. The cat stared down the alligator and occasionally batted its teeth-packed muzzle as the reptile tried to sneak the food. But the big fight was a draw because the alligator managed to snaffle some of the chicken before the brave moggy beat it off for good.

Too Sad to Sing

A parrot called Coco so loved singing with its mistress, Princess Charlotte of Wales, that when she died in 1817, the bird never sang again.

Cockpit Becomes Cat-Pit

A tabby cat cost a Canadian airline thousands of dollars when it escaped from its travel basket and delayed a flight for four hours in January 2012. Ripples was due to depart from Halifax, Nova Scotia, to Toronto when, most likely frightened, it wound up not just in the cockpit but lodged inside a panel of the airplane. Maintenance crews retrieved Ripples, who then had to endure the flight in the cold confines of the hold.

Pipsqueak Beats the Odds

A hamster had an incredible series of escapes in 2012 when its cage was broken into by a marauding cat. Not only did Siberian hamster Pipsqueak escape the cat's clutches but in its panicky flight across a busy main road it also avoided being run over, as well as the attentions of more cats and a dog. Owner Callum Chalkley, eight, had given up hope of ever seeing his hamster again when he went missing from the family home in Clifton, Hertfordshire but Pipsqueak was found taking refuge in the garage of a pest control contractor.

Picky Penguin

Pringle, a king penguin which lived at England's Chessington World of Adventures during the 1970s and 1980s, was rare for his species – he hated water. Also unusual for such sociable birds as penguins, he also loathed others of his kind.

Coming Bark to Life

A dog headed for the pub as his master lay injured and bleeding after a 12m (40ft) fall down a bank. But hero hound Monty knew this was the best place to get help for 73-year-old Maurice Holder. Monty barked and barked at a pub customer at Bodmin in Cornwall before leading a rescue party to the scene. Maurice had slipped down a cliff while on a walk but made a full recovery from his head and rib injuries.

Tiger Gets Grassed Up

Police had a severe shock in 2003 when they raided an apartment in the Harlem district of New York. After being confronted by the 180kg (400lb) Bengal tiger, which had a 0.9m (3ft) alligator for company, they beat a retreat almost as hastily as they had broken in!

Moose Loose – in the Air

Power workers didn't bargain for what they would discover when they investigated why the new cables they were hauling up were so taut. They went back to find that they had hauled a furious moose 15.4m (50½ft) into the air by its 5ft (1.5m) antlers. In the incident at the height of the rutting season near Fairbanks, Alaska, it would seem the agitated bull had thrashed around and got his antlers stuck in the cables when they were on the ground before being hauled into the air.